BEGIN WITH THE BRAIN

WITH THE

BRAIN

Second Edition

*This book is dedicated to my husband, Rick Burros, stepson, Greg Burros,
and my sons Kurt and Kris Kaufeldt.*

*Thank you for your love and support as I do the work
I am passionate about with other educators.*

BEGIN WITH THE BRAIN

Second Edition

Orchestrating the Learner-Centered Classroom

MARTHA KAUFELDT

CORWIN
A SAGE Ccmpany

For information:

Corwin
A SAGE Company
2455 Teller Road
Thousand Oaks, California 91320
(800) 233-9936
Fax: (800) 417-2466
www.corwinpress.com

SAGE Ltd.
1 Oliver's Yard
55 City Road
London EC1Y 1SP
United Kingdom

SAGE Pvt. Ltd.
B 1/I 1 Mohan Cooperative
 Industrial Area
Mathura Road, New Delhi 11C 044
India

SAGE Asia-Pacific Pte. Ltd.
33 Pekin Street #02-01
Far East Square
Singapore 048763

Printed in the United States of America

Library of Congress Cataloging-in-Publication Data

Begin with the brain : orchestrating the learner-centered classroom/editor, Martha Kaufeldt. — 2nd ed.
    p. cm.
Revised ed. of: Begin with the brain/Martha Kaufeldt.
Includes bibliographical references and index.
ISBN 978-1-4129-7157-7 (cloth)
ISBN 978-1-4129-7158-4 (pbk.)
    1. Learning, Psychology of. 2. Learning--Physiological aspects. 3. Brain. 4. Classroom environment. I. Kaufeldt, Martha, 1954- II. Kaufeldt, Martha, 1954- Begin with the brain. III. Title.

LB1057.K38 2010
370.15'23—dc22   2009028509

This book is printed on acid-free paper.

09 10 11 12 13 10 9 8 7 6 5 4 3 2 1

Acquisitions Editor:	Carol Chambers Collins
Associate Editor:	Julie McNall
Editorial Assistants:	Brett Ory and Allison Scott
Illustrators:	Mike Ericson and Judith Burros
Production Editor:	Veronica Stapleton
Copy Editor:	Adam Dunham
Typesetter:	C&M Digitals (P) Ltd.
Proofreader:	Dennis W. Webb
Cover Designer:	Scott Van Atta

Contents

Preface

Over a decade has passed since I began writing the first edition of *Begin With the Brain: Orchestrating the Learner-Centered Classroom.* At the time, I had just left my classroom teaching position and was launching my next career in professional development and teacher training.

We were in the midst of the so-called Decade of the Brain; the field of cognitive neuroscience was growing rapidly, and research studies were uncovering exciting new information about the human brain, much of it of profound interest to teachers. Some critics, however, felt that it was too early to base educational practice on the initial findings of cognitive neuroscience, and a few even suggested that *teachers* really weren't qualified to integrate the findings into classroom practice.

As a teacher working on the "front lines," I felt differently; for some years, I had been seeking out the research on my own, analyzing my own current practices and then creating new strategies based on what seemed to me to be commonsense adaptations of the best current research. Because of the positive results I'd achieved with my own students during these years of "action research," I became more and more certain that my experiences and strategies could provide valuable information to other educators. Since I'd already been integrating early brain research and practical teaching and learning strategies for years, I was proud to be part of the first generation of what was beginning to be known as the brain-based education movement. Today, I prefer to use the term *brain-compatible.* As Pat Wolfe and others have pointed out, the phrase *brain-based* implies the existence of other educational methods—such as *liver-based* or *intestine-based!*

In this revised and expanded edition of the original book, I continue to encourage and celebrate all of the commonsense strategies that can enhance a classroom environment, engage students, and promote meaningful learning. The reasons these techniques are successful, I believe, is that they reflect what science and recent research have concluded regarding the conditions for how human brains learn best and most efficiently. I want to take this opportunity to encourage educators to constantly reevaluate their current practices and see for themselves whether they are aligned with what we currently know about how our brains learn and remember. I would also urge teachers to modify the strategies they are using now to reflect the latest insights on how a student's brain might better be stimulated and engaged.

I realize that educators may never become "brain experts." I do maintain, however, that classroom teachers will continue to conduct valuable action research as they implement brain-compatible techniques—just as I did when I was a classroom teacher and continue to do when I work with adult learners.

Teaching, of course, is not a science, but an art. This new edition of *Begin With the Brain* is offered in support of the following proposition:

To maximize education, the art of teaching should be compatible with how brains learn.

Acknowledgments

When I wrote this book, I was overwhelmed by the realization of how as a teacher I have synthesized information and ideas from such a wide variety of people and sources. Throughout my career, I have had incredible associations and wonderful opportunities to work with gifted educators and researchers. As I attempted to compile and publish my strategies for success in the classroom, I was able to reflect on the various workshops, trainings, collaborations, and mentors from whom I have benefited.

In the area of brain research and learning theory, the following people have been instrumental in influencing me through their writings and in many cases their personal connections: Thomas Armstrong, Pat Belvel, Tony Buzan, Geoffrey and Renate Caine, Mihaly Csikszentmihalyi, Linda Darling-Hammond, Marion Diamond, David Elkind, Howard Gardner, Jeanne Gibbs, William Glasser, Daniel Goleman, Leslie Hart, Jane Healy, Eric Jensen, Spencer Kagan, Susan Kovalik, Alfie Kohn, Joseph LeDoux, Larry Lowery, Jane Nelsen, Candace Pert, Frank Smith, David Sousa, Robert Sylwester, Pat Wolfe, and Harry Wong. I encourage every educator to become a lifelong learner and investigate this growing field of knowledge.

As I added relevant cognitive neuroscience updates to this edition, I needed an expert to review and clarify some of the recent brain research. I was able to count on my friend and mentor for many years, Bob Sylwester, professor emeritus, author, speaker, and one of the most generous human beings on the planet, to offer his wise insights and deep knowledge on brainy stuff.

Over the years, there have been dozens of colleagues and friends who have been mentors and associates on a wide variety of projects. Robert Ellingsen, my dear friend and partner teacher at Monarch School, deserves special recognition as a collaborator, sounding board, innovator, tireless cohort, and absolutely dedicated educator!

Throughout this book, I refer frequently to Monarch Community School. It was during my tenure there that I learned, applied, tested, improved, and tweaked many of the tools I initially explored in this book. In the last 10 years, I have primarily been working as a teacher trainer and staff developer. To keep myself alert and aware of the current teaching profession, I have rotated into the classroom as a guest teacher or long-term substitute when I can. I have also taught summer school classes when I had newer strategies I wanted to implement and revise. I suspect I always learn far more from the students than they learn from me.

The first edition of this book was launched with the vision of Joey Tanner, former publisher at Zephyr Press, and the constant support, assistance, and encouragement of Veronica Durie, the managing editor. This second edition is now realized with the help of Carol Collins, Senior Editor, Brett Ory, and many others at Corwin Press.

A special thanks goes to LuLane Harrison, my trusty assistant for over 10 years, who always keeps things together when I am traveling and is my sounding board and friend.

I have been a member of the Burros family for eight years and continue to be amazed at the creative talents that so many of them possess. When I needed help the most, my new nephew-in-law Brandon Toropov, a brilliant author and editor, guided me through the last rewrite with his great insight and suggestions. My new sister-in-law, Judith Burros, an incredible artist in a variety of media, tackled the job of drawing me some brainy illustrations that beautifully add to this second edition. My husband, Rick Burros, kept me going with laughter and his sage advice when I was the most frustrated: "Cut it loose!"

Corwin gratefully acknowledges the contributions of the following reviewers:

Janice Bradley, PhD
Project Coordinator
New Mexico State
    University
Las Cruces, NM

Barbara Clark, EdD
Professor Emeritus
California State
    University, Los Angeles
Los Angeles, CA

Mari Gates
5th Grade Regular
    Education Inclusion
    Teacher
Henry B. Burkland
    Intermediate School
Middleboro, MA

Mike Scaddan
CEO, Brain Stems Ltd
Tauranga, New Zealand

Bess Scott, PhD
Director of Elementary
    Education
Lincoln Public Schools
Lincoln, NE

Leah Welte
Teacher
Alpine School District
American Fork, UT

About the Author

 **Martha Kaufeldt** began her teaching career in 1977. She has taught a variety of grades at the elementary level and language arts programs in middle school and high school. She began her research of brain-compatible teaching and learning strategies while working with several school districts to develop gifted, talented, and extended-learning programs. With a master's degree in human behavior, she believes that all educators should know more about how the brain learns. Martha continues to keep up to date on recent cognitive neuroscience research and incorporates new knowledge into her teaching practices and workshops. She considers herself a "brain research interpreter for educators."

In 1985, Martha designed and implemented a Concept-in-a-Day program to teach the concept of long division in a *single day*. This award-winning video documents an innovative immersion program and is used by teachers internationally. The success of the program introduced Martha as a powerful and dynamic workshop presenter.

Martha served as the Program Director, trainer, and coach for the Bay Area Middle Schools Project, and then during the 1992–1993 school year, Martha returned to the middle school classroom to get a reality check. As a seventh-grade humanities core teacher, Martha was able to work on an interdisciplinary teaching team implementing thematic curriculum. As a new challenge, Martha then worked for four years as the restructuring coordinator and the lead teacher at an alternative K–6 public elementary school in Santa Cruz, California. This unique program emphasized brain-compatible teaching strategies, differentiated instruction, multiage classes, authentic assessment, parent participation, and conflict resolution strategies. When her busy schedule allows it, Martha continues to rotate back into the classroom as a long-term substitute or guest teacher to help build up her "tackle box of strategies," and to remind her of the challenges educators face everyday in schools across North America.

Martha travels internationally giving energizing motivational presentations and dynamic workshops that address the fundamentals of brain-compatible learning theory, differentiated instruction, classroom management, and assessment for all grade levels. Martha's unique experiences and background have provided her with many examples and suggestions for teachers who are ready to hear about the incredible possibilities that await their students. She is also the author of *Teachers, Change Your Bait! Brain-Compatible Differentiated Instruction* (2005). Martha can be reached at Martha@beginwiththebrain.com or on her Web site at www.beginwiththebrain.com.

Introduction

Brain-Compatible Learning and Learner-Centered Education

Brain-compatible teaching occurs when educators seek out an understanding of current cognitive neuroscience research, translate specific findings into holistic practical strategies, and incorporate those strategies into their classroom practice. All decisions regarding instructional strategies, curriculum design, learning environments, and even behavior management can be influenced by what we know is *compatible* with how the brain learns optimally. While much of the neuroscience research may be in its infancy or specific to unique situations, the new knowledge can provide teachers with insight into the behaviors, learning abilities, skill acquisition, and emotional development of students. The research is confirming what great teachers have known intuitively:

- Students must feel safe and secure to maximize their ability to engage.
- Novelty and joyfulness contribute to engagement.
- Predictable patterns for behaviors and tasks can assist learners to know what to do next.
- Multisensory experiences in enriched environments can enhance brain growth and development.
- New concepts are acquired more quickly if they are hooked to prior learning and experiences.

1

- Processing new knowledge in a variety of ways can increase retention.
- Every learner is unique and has specific learning preferences and styles.

The human brain is dynamic and constantly reshaping itself based on its environment and experiences throughout life. This knowledge should influence parents and educators regarding everything they say or do—or don't do—as they contribute to the development of young brains. At the very least, some basic understanding of brain research can not only help teachers realize what teaching methods can *maximize* learning but also what methods might *minimize* learning.

Important information about how our brains grow, learn, forget, develop, diminish, and create is now being uncovered every day. Thanks to imaging tools such as fMRI (functional magnetic resonance imaging), new knowledge and understanding about the mysterious three-pound organ between our ears is being discovered and documented at an exponential rate—a speed that was inconceivable just a decade ago. Thousands of books, hundreds of Web sites, and dozens of education conferences are now dedicated to the seemingly inexhaustible subject: how the brain learns.

Many writers who follow the research in neuroscience, psychiatry, neurophysiology, nutrition, sociology, behavioral and cognitive psychology, and other fields have provided translational approaches to applying scientific findings in the classroom. Some researchers suggest that current neuroscience research findings are too preliminary and contradictory for educators to take the risk of interpreting and applying them to classroom practice. While I respect the rigor and cautionary stance of these experts, I cannot agree with their suggestion that teachers should ignore what we have recently learned about brain function. In many cases, brain-compatible teaching techniques are commonsense, natural learning strategies that excellent educators have used intuitively for years.

As research progresses and new complex studies emerge, the translation into the educational area must be dynamic also. Over the years, in order to point out the practical applicability of brain research, many trainers and authors, myself included, have suggested simple techniques to begin creating a brain-friendly classroom. Some teachers implemented just a handful of ideas (such as altering the lights, providing water bottles, playing background music, or organizing brain-energizing movement activities) and then professed to be providing a comprehensive learning program based on the latest brain research! As time has passed and more information has become available, I believe that a more in-depth approach is now easier to support. Many teachers are now ready to explore more fully the question of how cognitive neuroscience can influence all aspects of curriculum and enrich instructional strategies. Through staff development, professional learning communities, and readings and investigations, educators are catching and riding a wave of new knowledge to apply in daily classroom implementation.

Learner-Centered Education

I believe that adjusting teaching strategies, designing safe and secure learning environments, and creating body-compatible classrooms should now be classified as *brain-compatible* techniques. Perhaps just as important, they should be seen as examples of *learner-centered* education.

This term emphasizes the importance of paying careful attention to the prior knowledge, existing skills, cultural differences, attitudes, and beliefs that learners bring to the educational environment. Learner-centered classrooms use instructional design and teaching practices based on what is currently known about learning and cognition. Such practices create environments where the individual student's needs, abilities, and interests are the primary focus.

> The learner-centered approach encourages the student to be responsible for his or her own learning, emphasizes cooperation, addresses learning differences, and even considers each student's unique response to stress and pressure.

Teaching is always a matter of doing what you can with what you know at the time. I remember a year early in my career when I had 38 students in a single fourth- and fifth-grade class. These kids were creative, energetic, silly, devious, wired, curious, and fun. In 180 days I was supposed to teach them *all* their required subjects! I had to use every strategy I could think of just to keep us on track. I approached this task as I had approached similar situations in my teaching career: by giving points and time-outs, by taking away privileges, personal property, and rights. I controlled and dictated, mandated and glared. I used stopwatches, stickers, tickets, and "bucks." Most of the strategies were for a good reason at the time, and many of them seemed to work for a while. Many were just desperate attempts to control the chaos.

When I finally began investigating the research about the brain and learning, I found out that I was able to understand many of the possible reasons for my students' actions and behaviors. Once I understood the theory, I could create systems that were more likely to prevent the situations that kept students from being as successful as they could be.

I believe the most successful teachers have always used learner-centered, brain-compatible strategies intuitively. What makes the present period so exciting is that we now have a better understanding of why those great teachers' get such good results!

As I conduct teacher workshops, I always ask participants to review all of the ideas that I suggest and identify the ones they are already using in their classroom practice. Invariably, people spot brain-compatible, learner-centered strategies they've been incorporating successfully in the classroom.

"That's great!" I say whenever we identify one of these strategies. "Give yourself a pat on the back!" I also ask teachers to reflect on their typical teaching day and consider routines and situations that may now be a struggle for their students.

A thoughtful, responsive teacher is always on the lookout for innovative ways to improve and on the lookout for new ideas. Today's brain research allows us to confirm and elaborate on some truly great ideas for teachers. Thanks to the remarkable research that's taken place in recent years, we are now in a position to orchestrate much more effective strategies for our students. Isn't that our job? I believe it is, and I believe a brain-compatible, learner-centered classroom can become a reality for our students once we begin to understand just a little bit of what is now known about how the brain functions, learns, and reacts.

New Material

It is possible to be overwhelmed with available information and resources when one begins to seek an understanding on how the brain learns. Included in this new edition are several brief updates on brain research as it applies to education. Hopefully, these "Brain Basics" may motivate you to expand your own knowledge. Some of you may be interested in the actual research and neurobiology. Educators are often most interested in practical applications of the research. At the end of each "Brain Basics" section, I have included recommendations of favorite books and online resources that pertain to the topic described. I hope these suggestions will encourage you to take the next step in understanding your students' and your own brains.

This book is *not* designed to make you a brain expert. Instead, it is designed to be like the great teacher down the hall, the teacher from whom you can get lots of ideas for orchestrating and maintaining a harmonious classroom. Maybe you already know a teacher you are comfortable asking for advice right now—advice on how to create a learning environment that is both joyous and rigorous, on how to help students understand and buy into classroom standards and procedures you set up together, or how to get students thinking of themselves as part of a team. I hope that this book will become one of your great teachers down the hall—a teacher with some core insights on how the brain functions and reliably good advice on how to minimize stress and fear in the classroom, how to maximize positive interactions, and how to approach students on their own terms. If, along the way, you learn more about how the human brain functions, so much the better.

The ideas and approaches to classroom instruction and management that I share in this book are

- Linked to current research regarding how human brains think, learn, and respond to the environment;
- Respectful of the individual learner's background, prior knowledge, culture, individual interests, and experiences;
- Based on my own years as a successful classroom teacher and my own observations of dynamic colleagues;

- Designed to diminish "learned helplessness" in students and promote confidence, initiative, and motivation; and
- Meant to be used in creative ways, modified as needed, and not implemented as a "magic bullet."

"Don't smile until Christmas!" a master teacher told me in the mid-1970s. "Show 'em who's boss and don't back down . . . otherwise you'll lose control and it'll all be over."

Oh, brother!

I am a veteran teacher, having taught at all grade levels. I began my readings and research on the brain and learning theory in 1980 and have been applying brain-based learning concepts in my classrooms ever since. I *know* that there are a variety of ways that educators can organize their classrooms that will make them effective, productive, and most of all *joyous* places for learning to take place. My first suggestion is to *smile*.

1

Begin With the Brain

Interpreting Neuroscience Research

It is often popularly argued that advances in the understanding of brain development and mechanisms of learning have substantial implications for education and the learning sciences. . . . Neuroscience has advanced to the point where it is time to think critically about the form in which research information is made available to educators so that it is interpreted appropriately for practice.

—Bransford, et al., *How People Learn*

In the early 1980s I heard Dr. Marian Diamond, a neuroscientist from the University of California at Berkeley, give a keynote address at the annual conference for the California Association for the Gifted. After she had amazed the audience of primarily educators with her findings about "enriched environments," brain "plasticity," and the implications for students, she asked the most profound question, to which I still have not discovered a reasonable answer:

"If the brain is the organ for learning, then why aren't teachers brain experts?"

Twenty-five years ago, I suppose we could put our naïve heads in the sand and profess that the latest brain research, including Dr. Diamond's, was most often based on studies done on rats, sea slugs, and primates. The research didn't yet prove anything about human brains. Now, we can't ignore the incredible discoveries of the last three decades about the brain mechanisms that influence learning and memory:

- Advancements in neuroimaging techniques have allowed researchers to get a glimpse of the brain's activity as people perform tasks.
- Neurobiologists are helping us understanding the brain's chemistry and the influences of genetics and the environment—nature *and* nurture.
- Cognitive neuroscience research sheds light on the impact of emotions on learning and socialization.
- Neurophysiology studies demonstrate the importance of movement, exercise, and nutrition.

As the research surfaced during the 1990s, known as the Decade of the Brain, many noteworthy folks stepped up to the plate to help interpret the findings for the education community. Geoffrey and Renate Nummela Caine, Leslie Hart, Robert Sylwester, Eric Jensen, David Sousa, Susan Kovalik, Robin Fogarty, and Kay Burke were some of the first to refer to brain-compatible learning: the purposeful planning of classrooms, climate, and curriculum around what we knew about how the brain works best.

With the advent of neuroimaging devices in the 1970s (such as PET scans), we began a new journey—one that took scientists for the first time into the inner sanctum of the human brain *during* the process of learning. . . . Finally, some of what we have known intuitively all along can now be substantiated. Some teaching methods *discourage* quality learning, just as some clearly *encourage* it. (Jensen & Dabney, 2000, p. xi)

In pursuing the answer to Dr. Diamond's important question, I've found out from direct experience that some teachers, while not brain experts in any formal sense, do teach in a way that supports what I will call a *brain-compatible* classroom. In this chapter, I'll begin to show you what they're doing right—usually without even realizing it. We've all run into teachers we admire and want to emulate, teachers who get truly extraordinary results from their students. What I've learned is that these great teachers are, very often, teaching in accordance with some of the most advanced findings on the workings of the human brain.

One of the best original summaries for brain-compatible learning (also referred to as *brain-based* learning) is by Geoffrey and Renate Caine (1994) in their book *Making Connections: Teaching and the Human Brain.* In one of their more recent books, coauthored with Carol McClintic and Karl Klimek (2005), *12 Brain/Mind Principles in Action,* they state that,

We argue that on the basis of research and experience that meaningful learning occurs when three elements are intertwined: A state of mind in learners that we call relaxed alertness, the orchestrated immersion of the learner in experiences in which the standards are imbedded, and the active processing of that experience." (p. xiii)

For the last 12 years, I have adapted these three elements, first referred to by the Caines, and developed them into three basic categories of brain research that can influence educational practices. These big ideas about how we can optimize learning based on neuroscience research are what the rest of this

BEGIN WITH THE BRAIN BASICS

Brain Basics

The human brain consists of over 100 billion neurons and about a trillion much smaller glial support cells. The two types of cells split the mass of our brain. Glial cells are not directly involved in information transmission but provide the support and maintenance of the neurons and their trillions of synapses: the points where each connection is made.

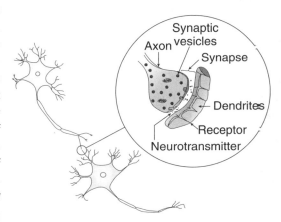

Each neuron has a *cell body;* multiple *dendrites* that branch out and grow with stimulation, forming the gray matter; and a single *axon* that typically develops *myelin,* a white fatty insulation, ending with a collection of *synaptic terminals.* Neurons communicate through an intricate network of electrochemical interactions. An electrical charge called the *action potential* is generated within the cell running from the dendrites through the axon to the *synapse,* the point of contact with another neuron. The myelin sheath acts as an insulator and assures that the charge reaches its goal.

The actual communication between neurons is a biochemical interaction. A variety of *neurotransmitters* are stored in vesicles at the base of each axon terminal, and with the arrival of the action potential, they are released to travel across the gap to attach to receptor sites on the other side of the *synaptic cleft* (gap). As the postsynaptic receptors are stimulated, another action potential is generated within that neuron, starting a chain reaction of firing

Neurons create columns of connections, complex pathways, and form intricate networks and brain systems (see Neuroplasticity, page 13, and Use It or Lose It, pages 14–15). These circuits transport sensory and motor signals to all areas of the body. Specialized regions and lobes are dedicated to movement, sensory input, language, hearing and vision, and so on. The prefrontal lobe, largest in humans, is considered the executive area as it coordinates and integrates the work of all the other regions.

The average adult brain weighs about three pounds. The consistency is like a cube of unrefrigerated butter or cream cheese. It consumes about 20% of the body's energy when at rest. The internal layers of the brain are surrounded by cerebral spinal fluid that acts as a watery cushion.

Research: The Executive Brain by Elkonon Goldberg, Oxford Univ. Press, 2001.

Practical Application: Magic Trees of the Mind by Marian Diamond & Janet Hopson, Penguin Books, 1998.

Web Site: The Lundbeck Institute: http://www.brainexplorer.org/brain_atlas/Brainatlas_index.shtml

book is based on. The strategies included in the following chapters can all be clustered within at least one of these *three key elements.*

Three Key Elements of Brain-Compatible Teaching and Learning

1. Less Stress: ⭐
*Create a Safe and Secure Climate
and Environment to Reduce Perceived
Threat and Danger*

The main task here is to create a climate and environment that are conducive to learning by creating a balance of "low threat" and "high challenge" (the Caines use the term *Relaxed Alertness*).

To create a state of mind that is optimal for meaningful learning, the most important factors are

- Maintaining an atmosphere of trust and respect, where perceived threat is low and balanced with high challenge (i.e., a sense of safety and security that encompasses the mental, emotional, and physical levels);
- Keeping learning joyful and yet rigorous;
- Making sure students know the agenda, purpose, and game plan to reduce anticipatory anxiety;
- Creating a physically healthy and safe environment (sound, light, temperature, basic needs, etc.);
- Orchestrating a socially safe atmosphere where a sense of inclusion is fostered and conflict resolution strategies are demonstrated and utilized;
- Allowing time for reflection, contemplation, and expansion to process new information; and
- Teaching coping strategies for dealing with everyday stress, including stressors from home and outside of school.

If the stress response is activated, it can minimize the brain's capabilities to learn and remember. The best curriculum and instructional strategies will be useless if the student is in the *reflex response.* Later in this chapter, I will explain how this physiological reaction takes place and how to orchestrate strategies to avoid it.

2. Do the Real Thing!
Provide Meaningful Multisensory Experiences in an Enriched Environment

According to *Making Connections* (Caine & Caine, 1994), the thrust here is to "take information off the page and the blackboard and bring it to life in the minds of students" (p. 115). The focus is on how students are exposed to content (the Caines refer to this as *Orchestrated Immersion*). A strong emphasis should be on creating themes and real-world connections around which fragmented curriculum topics can be organized. Students must then have opportunities to do their learning through multisensory, complex, real projects. Classrooms must be environments that combine the planning of key experiences for students and, at the same time, with the opportunity for spontaneity. Experiences must be aligned with students' developmental stages and prior knowledge. Multisensory, real-world experiences actually promote brain growth and development. Teachers need to

- Pre-assess students' prior experiences and background knowledge;
- Determine if the content and concept is developmentally appropriate;
- Provide complex, interactive, first-hand learning experiences;
- Make sure content is meaningful and relevant (hook concepts to prior knowledge);
- Provide a wide variety of input and resources; and
- Allow adequate time!

Research on brain plasticity is profound. When exposed to stimulation, the neurons in our brains are prompted to grow dendritic branches that reach out and connect with other neurons. Simply put, this neural network that develops is where our thoughts and memories are "stored."

BEGIN WITH THE BRAIN BASICS

Neuro "Plasticity"

When the brain is exposed to multisensory stimulation in an enriched environment, neurons are prompted to grow dendritic branches and form new synaptic connections with other neurons. The "father" of the biology of learning and memory, Eric Kandel, was awarded a Nobel Prize in Medicine in 2000 for his early discoveries about neuroplasticity and memory. He discovered that when people learn something, the wiring in their brain changes. Dr. Marian Diamond's (UC Berkeley) pioneering research proved that environmental enrichment could influence and change the structure of the brain by increasing the cerebral cortex. Her work indicated that being exposed to enriched environments and stimulation could enrich brains at any age.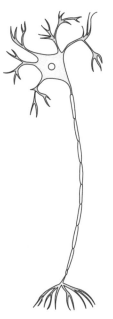

When babies are born, many neural connections are already in place. By the time children are 10 years old, there will have been a tremendous growth period where some regions of the brain create three times as many connections as they will have later as adults. The brain then goes through a period of intense pruning (arborization). With the onset of puberty, there is another growth surge and subsequent pruning period. While there are basic developmental tendencies and time frames for growth, each brain becomes uniquely wired and shaped. There are some connections that are "experience independent," which means that you are hard wired at birth or have a genetic predisposition (*nature*). Then there is "experience dependent" brain wiring that will occur only when we are exposed to experiences that prompt the new dendritic growth and synaptic connections (*nurture*). No two brains are wired in exactly the same way. Every brain is uniquely formed.

Research: In Search of Memory by Eric R. Kandel, W.W. Norton & Co., 2006.

Practical Application: How the Brain Learns by David Sousa, Corwin, 2005.

Web Site: The Brain Connection http://www.brainconnection.positscience.com

When we have stimulating experiences that are appropriate for our level of development, our brains can grow rapidly. In classrooms, I call this the "Aha! moment." Marcia Tate's (2003) popular book, *Worksheets Don't Grow Dendrites!*, puts forth the theory that active learning will develop brains and thinking more effectively than a more passive, paper-pencil, worksheet approach.

★3. Use It or Lose It!
Actively Process New Concepts in a Variety of Ways to Assure Long-Term Retention

In order for students to make sense of an experience, they must have some opportunities to do active processing. "To fully capitalize on experience, there should be 'in the moment,' ongoing consolidation that solidifies and expands knowledge" (Caine, Caine, McClintic, & Klimek, 2005, p. 6). This process can encourage students to develop and express creative insights as it allows them to take charge of their own learning. By reflecting and extending a learning experience, the student strengthens the initial brain connections and builds long-term retention.

An environment that promotes the Use It or Lose It principle

- Structures frequent opportunities for students to *reflect* on the product and process of their learning. In a brain-compatible learning environment, students are provided opportunities to learn not only about the subject in question but also about themselves as people. Learners need time to contemplate and to get feedback from others as they process the learning experiences in a variety of ways so that they might adequately grasp the implications.

- Provides daily activities that allow students personal *choice* in how they process and store new knowledge. You become automatically *engaged* if you have to make a choice of any kind. In a brain-compatible learning environment, students should have multiple opportunities to discover and process information based on their preferred learning styles. There should be inquiries, activities, and projects that address a variety of critical thinking levels and the students' multiple intelligences. Choice activities should facilitate students' understanding of key concepts and can also be used as authentic assessment tools. Students can be guided to make activity choices that are challenging for them. Providing choice opportunities demands active processing and builds self-esteem and confidence.

BEGIN WITH THE BRAIN BASICS

Use It or Lose It

Multisensory input stimulates neurons to fire, starting a chain reaction within a neural network. Learning enhances and builds the synaptic connections by requiring more activity. With increased activity at the synapse, the greater the attraction, and the electrochemical signals begin to fire more quickly and easily. This developing quick response is called long term potentiation (LTP). The more a neuron is called on to be involved, the chemical and electrical responses grow more likely to fire with less stimulation. Like neuroscientists say, "Neurons that fire together, wire together."

Newly formed synapses are fragile. Learning requires strengthening the affinity between the neurons. The more activity, the stronger the attraction becomes. With more stimulation, glutamate (a neurotransmitter) is produced in the axon and triggers a connection at the synapse. New research has identified proteins called brain-derived neurotrophic factors (BDNF) that build and maintain the cell circuitry and health.

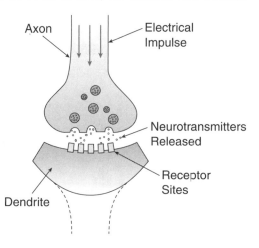

Dr. John Ratey (2008) refers to BDNF as the Miracle-Gro® for your neurons. Exercise and improved circulation has been discovered as the best way to elevate the levels of BDNF in one's brain.

During several early developmental stages of brain growth, there is an overproduction of synapses. It is estimated that at age 12, there may be 125% of the synaptic connections that will be present at adulthood. As the brain begins to specialize, it prunes and limits the number of successful synapses that will remain. The arborization process happens naturally throughout life and is part of normal development.

With purposeful stimulation the connections are strengthened and are less likely to experience apoptosis (natural cell "suicide" due to lack of stimulation). Some research on sleep indicates that during REM periods the brain restimulates the important (meaningful) connections and that other periods of sleep may be the necessary downtime for pruning to occur. Studies have shown that the brain actually recycles the underused pruned dendrites and uses the material as building blocks for new dendrite growth.

Research: SPARK: The Revolutionary New Science of Exercise and the Brain by John Ratey, MD, Little, Brown, 2008.

Practical Application: Enriching the Brain by Eric Jensen, Jossey-Bass, 2006.

Web Site: Bio-Medicine: http://www.bio-medicine.org/Biology-Definition/Synapse

- Orchestrates a variety of *collaboration* opportunities. In a brain-compatible learning environment, students have multiple opportunities to acquire and practice communication and social skills. Working together on projects builds a sense of community and encourages meaningful conversations and reflections. Students begin to have successful experiences in working together toward a common goal. The sharing of knowledge and experiences among students is an essential element of brain-compatible learning.

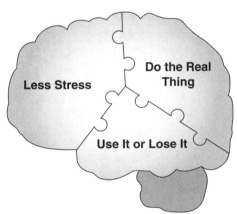

As a result, brain-compatible learning must involve:

- Designing and orchestrating lifelike, enriching, and appropriate experiences for learning in a safe and secure environment.
- Ensuring that students process in such a way as to increase the extraction of meaning.

I now recognize that in my early days of teaching many of my lessons and strategies were actually quite "brain-antagonistic!" For lack of a better plan or rationale, I had students seated in rows of desks, forbidden to speak to each other, as I asked them to memorize pages of facts that were more about the "long ago and far away" than the "here and now" of their worlds. I depended on the textbook to make connections and trudged through it all in an effort to "cover the curriculum." My first glimpse of students in a natural learning mode was when I took my sixth graders to a weeklong outdoor education camp. There, my students were exposed to real-world experiences in a safe and secure enriched environment that brought out the joy of learning! I was challenged! How could I bring this engagement and excitement back to a classroom environment? I knew there had to be a way!

For many educators, brain-compatible learning means a major paradigm shift in their teaching methods and styles. They need to go beyond providing information and requiring the memorization of isolated facts and skills. In a brain-compatible learning environment, educators must orchestrate the experiences for the students so they can extract understanding and meaningfulness for themselves. The most important aspect for educators to consider is that the brain is constantly searching for how things make sense, based on what the learner already knows and values. The brain is always looking to detect patterns and relationships and, in essence, seeking order out of chaos. Meaningfulness and building on students' prior experiences should become central issues for teachers as they rethink how learning takes place.

> Knowledge about the brain alone cannot provide a blueprint for how to educate. Information about brain development can assist only in educational design, which is no less a creative act than is the design of a bridge or a new factory. (Posner & Rothbart, 2007, p. 3)

From Fear to Flow: Maximizing the Brain's Capabilities

The most recent brain research confirms that encountering perceived threat and stress in the environment inhibits the brain and minimizes its capabilities. If the brain must deal with frustration, fear, or confusion, its performance is inhibited, which results in students' feeling helpless. Conversely, appropriate challenges and some degree of pressure enhance the brain's potential. Each individual is unique and will respond to challenge or threat in a unique way, but generally, humans are able to engage in optimal experiences in environments where there is a balance between challenge and low threat.

The classroom climate and environment must be designed with learning in mind. A classroom that is physically uncomfortable or maintains a threatening atmosphere or tone will minimize students' brains' abilities to function at their highest potential. Understanding some of the latest research about how our brain reacts to stress and fear can help teachers know what *not* to do and begin to know what *to* do.

BEGIN WITH THE BRAIN BASICS

Stress and Learning

When we experience a dangerous or stressful situation, or we *perceive* that we are being threatened, our brain's default system for emergencies kicks into high gear. The amygdala, two almond-shaped structures located in the mid-brain or limbic area, trigger the brain and body to react with the appropriate "fight-flight-freeze" response to a crisis with the release of high levels of stress hormones such as adrenaline and cortisol. When this reflexive automatic action takes over, the executive reflective functions of the brain's prefrontal lobes are temporarily bypassed as we respond to the danger or threat at hand. Once the immediacy of the situation has been taken care of, higher-level thinking strategies can be considered. Thoughtful solutions and a plan of action can be implemented.

Under chronic stress and perceived threat, the flood of adrenaline can begin to cause long-term cardiovascular and other immune-system problems, and high levels of cortisol can eventually damage cells in the hippocampus, affecting learning and memory. Prolonged stress can lead to learned helplessness and eventually chronic depression.

On the other hand, a healthy level of released cortisol energizes our brain for engagement. When we notice something that piques our interest or challenges our abilities, our motivation increases and we focus our attention. Mild stress and pressure can therefore enhance learning and memory. The challenge is finding the "sweet spot," as Daniel Goleman (2006) refers to the peak of "optimal cognitive efficiency," for each individual.

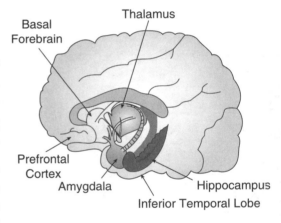

Research: Synaptic Self by Joseph LeDoux, Penguin Group, 2002.

Practical Applications: Social Intelligence by Daniel Goleman, Bantam Dell, 2006.

Web Resource: The Whalen Lab—Department of Psychology and Brain Sciences at Dartmouth College: http://www.whalenlab.info/Links.html

Identifying Triggers of Defensive Behaviors

The brain responds to fear with defensive behaviors to maximize the possibility of surviving dangerous situations in the most beneficial way. The brain's attentional system is wired to be alert to patterns and signs in the environment that may indicate danger and threat. Not only does the brain respond to dangers that our ancestors experienced, such as quick movements, loud sounds, bright lights, and predators, but each brain also has a unique set of past experiences. These personal memories of traumatic circumstances sometimes intrude into our everyday life. We filter our present situations through such memories, which often biases our interpretation. In our classrooms, we often see students react to situations based on their prior experiences. If we look, act, or speak like an adult with whom a student has had a fearful experience, then he might assume we will mistreat him as did that individual. If a student has had problems with the writing process, she may confuse new writing tasks with prior failures. Of course, the difficulty here is that every human has a unique set of experiences, so a situation that one person might perceive as threatening will not necessarily threaten another.

When the brain perceives threat in the environment, or feels stressed, anxious, or out of control, it sends messages through the nervous system to the body and regulates the various organs to try to match the demands of the situation at hand. This adrenaline surge can occur whether our body faces physical, environmental, or emotional danger, or academic confusion and frustration. An upset stomach, a racing heart, high blood pressure, clammy hands, and a dry mouth are all signs of fear in humans.

Reflexive and Reflective

For more than two decades, this phenomenon was referred to as *downshifting*. This term grew out of Paul MacLean's (see Caine & Caine, 1994, ch. 5, p. 57) triune brain theory and is meant to suggest that when under a perceived threat the human brain gears down to the brain stem to react to the danger at the expense of other areas of the brain. However, more recent neurological research has proved that the triune brain theory is simplistic at best and erroneous at worst. Robert Sylwester (1998), a well-known author, university professor, and synthesizer of brain research, suggests that this metaphor doesn't fully represent how our brain's complex response systems really work. Sylwester proposes that we use the terms *reflexive* and *reflective* to describe the two separate response systems in the brain.

As information from our senses comes into the brain, it does an instantaneous and crude evaluation of the input. It quickly compares what is being perceived in the context of prior memories and experiences that it has on file. Our body responds *reflexively* to the possible alarm, whether it is a physical threat, emotional stress, environmental danger, or academic confusion and frustration. If the sensory input either matches a negative memory or is an unknown and does not compute with any prior experiences, then the brain sounds off the 911 alert. This alert sparks the brain to produce a survival response and triggers an immediate adrenaline reaction. The brain gets the body ready to execute a possible defense: heart rhythms and blood pressure increase, stress hormones are released into the bloodstream, and perspiration begins.

The sensory information about the perceived danger or threat also travels, often simultaneously, to the cortex for a more rational evaluation. When the cortex considers the situation, it might confirm that the situation is threatening, that indeed, there is a reason to react. But if this more thoughtful *reflection* suggests that we have overreacted, the brain may send out a message to counteract the reflexive message. It can turn off the adrenaline push and call off the drill. It releases the appropriate hormones to counteract the adrenal surge.

Shifting From Reaction to Action

The *reaction* phenomenon often narrows our focus to survival only, what I refer to as "going into 911 mode." This fast, stress-driven system activates early-programmed methods of dealing with danger or perceived threats: hitting, screaming, running, crying, hiding, and so on. But as Sylwester (1998) points out, the reflexive behaviors should not be viewed as necessarily negative. We have reflexive behaviors that are positive responses. When we react quickly—reaching to catch the glass as it tips over, slamming on the brakes for the animal in the road, getting pumped up to run a race—we are using primitive responses and programmed behaviors as appropriate responses to the conditions.

Fight or Flight

When facing a perceived threat, our brain sets aside creativity, mental rehearsal, and complex thinking and puts in place predictable, easy-to-implement survival behaviors. Don't think—just do it! When a reflexive response occurs because of exposure to a perceived threat, true danger, or stress, most human brains are less capable of doing any of the following:

Stops!

- Being creative
- Seeing or hearing environmental clues
- Remembering and accessing prior learning
- Engaging in complex tasks, open-ended thinking, and questioning
- Sorting to filter out unimportant data
- Planning and mentally rehearsing
- Detecting patterns
- Communicating effectively
- Engaging in complex intellectual tasks

I recall that as I used my old computer, I would often run out of accessible memory (RAM). I would get a message on the screen that said I needed to close some applications or windows before I could open new applications. I simply could not do everything at once, and my computer demanded that I use and keep open only the windows that were absolutely necessary. Today's computers have changed the screen messages, but the same basic process still plays out. If you try to do too many things at once with the computer, it may limit or delay your ability to start something new. (Now on my Macintosh computer I might see the spinning "beach ball of death" as the system processes my many demands.) In effect, the same thing often goes on in the brain when it reacts to a perceived threat; other windows and applications will be temporarily closed so that the available RAM can be devoted to the defense reflex.

Common reflex triggers are

- Survival issues, dangerous situations
- Perceived threat and stress
- Old memories of danger or stressful situations
- Unfamiliar circumstances or unknown agenda
- Chaos, confusion, sensory overload

Common physiological responses are

- Surge of stress hormones
- Startle reflex
- Increased blood pressure and rapid, shallow breathing
- Upset stomach, dry mouth
- The neck and shoulders (the hackles) and large muscle groups stimulated

Although these useful automatic reactions are meant for survival, the physiological responses to perceived threats and the necessity of reacting to them over time might also create a sense of lethargy and fatigue. Studies show chronic stress can result in a depressed immune system, which can cause students to get sick more frequently. James E. Zull (2002), in his book *The Art of Changing the Brain,* describes how intense feelings and stress can begin to damage long-term memory. Extreme stress can permanently damage our memory centers, as in cases of PTSD (post-traumatic stress disorder) and childhood abuse.

Stress damages the hippocampus, leading to a shrinkage of dendrites and ultimately cell death. Not surprisingly, functions that depend on the hippocampus, like explicit or declarative memory, become severely compromised . . . and make [neurons] less capable of performing their job in the face of stringent demands. (LeDoux, 2002, p. 278)

Even as we defensively react to stress or threat, we size up the situation and create a plan. The brain shifts from reaction to action. As Joseph LeDoux (1996) explains, "In responding first with its most-likely-to-succeed behavior, the brain buys time" (p. 175). An instantaneous survival response such as *fight, flight*, or *freeze* doesn't demand any careful consideration or choices to be made. You simply *react*.

Eventually you take control. You make a plan and carry it out. This requires that your cognitive resources be directed to the emotional problem. You have to stop thinking about whatever you were thinking about before the danger occurred and start thinking about the danger you are facing (and already responding to automatically). (p. 176)

We quickly review various options and recall previous successes. We predict possible outcomes and prioritize the steps that we want to take. We thoughtfully plan the voluntary action that we want to take to replace the involuntary reaction that saved us initially and bought us some time.

As teachers, we work to reduce the conditions in our students' environments that induce the reflex response. At the same time, we must help students acquire personal strategies to deal with stress. Teaching students strategies that might help them when they are exposed to perceived threat or true danger should be incorporated into daily lessons. I have taught a series of lessons to students called "The Stress Mess." I ask them to reflect on the types of things that might cause them to go into a reflex response when at school. They are encouraged to illustrate these "demons." We then take time to discuss what strategies the teacher might apply to lessen the stress levels of students. We also begin categorizing the coping skills that successful students use to deal with anticipatory anxiety, test pressure, grades, performances, and so on.

The lessons can help students identify what things stress them out at school and home and what to do about it. Students can begin to identify what causes them to feel stressed or threatened and begin to build a repertoire of ways to cope with and manage that stress. Teaching students about stress and providing practice with patterns of responses will help them learn appropriate actions to take when they are stressed. The healthier the coping patterns that students store, the more possibilities from which they can choose. The following chapters will share a variety of strategies to help students:

- Manage time and schedules;
- Build communication techniques;
- Nurture healthy relationships;
- Participate in conflict resolution;
- Solve problems;
- Develop creativity and divergent thinking;
- Make thoughtful decisions and choices;
- Manage anger and emotional upsets;
- Practice self-reflection and relaxation; and
- Enhance health and nutrition.

Fear and Threat at School

What things at school might students perceive as threats, so they respond reflexively, minimizing their capabilities? We know that all students and situations are unique. Some middle and high school students may feel constantly threatened by other students who are gang members. At other campuses, the pressure of grades, awards, competitions, and social standing may cause students to feel stressed. Elementary schools may have bullies, verbally abusive students, and certain kids who dominate others. Even schools with no obvious social problems may have extremely complex schedules and rotations. Many young children may find this kind of atmosphere confusing or even threatening. Students in schools where a variety of languages are spoken in the homes or that have high migrant populations may feel threatened by communication difficulties and possible lack of long-standing relationships. Just being in an environment with hundreds of others may trigger some students to feel threatened.

As a teacher, I have witnessed students reacting defensively in the classroom. Test anxiety is a classic example. It is often marked by a physical reflex response: upset stomach, perspiration, and agitation. The brain is actually trying to react to the threat by keeping the students ready. For some students, the reflex response is so overwhelming that it keeps them from performing well on the exam. This reflex response also happens for many students when they are auditioning for a part in the school play, giving an oral report to the class, or even reading aloud. I have seen students become highly emotional or defensive when they are assigned a new book or moved to the next level in a curriculum program. These students respond reflexively to anything new because they perceive a pattern of failure.

But besides performances or evaluation situations, there are day-to-day events that seem to cause many students to have this reaction. Students may feel threatened by a parent if they don't perform well in school or receive a certain grade. This overwhelming threat may actually cause them to perform worse. Students who have an "over-scheduled" life often exhibit signs of stress.

Students' perceptions of whether or not the classroom is a safe and secure environment can influence their reactions. A long-term relationship with a teacher appears to strengthen feelings of safety and reduce anxiety. Other factors seem to relate to personality. Shy, sensitive children often react defensively to some of the most simple assignments and challenges. Students who are risk takers in general might react positively to stress or threat.

It is not difficult to generate a list of conditions under which your students are likely to respond reflexively. Although several of the circumstances listed below could challenge or pressure certain students to perform well, many students are threatened by these events; consider them carefully:

- Fear of potential physical harm from teachers or other students
- Emotional threats, embarrassment, put-downs, demonstrated disrespect for self, culture, or social group
- Inadequate time to complete a task
- Lack of time for reflection and expansion
- Predetermined correct outcomes established by an external agent
- Unfamiliar work with little support for learning
- Lack of orderliness and coherence
- Physical and social isolation
- Unknown purpose, schedule, or agenda
- Lack of information about a task, behavior expectations, or goals
- Punishments for failure, such as loss of privileges
- Competitions and contests
- Extrinsic rewards
- Perceived irrelevance and lack of personal meaning
- Restricted movement and lack of physical activity

As I noted earlier, using some of these occasionally with some situations may in fact be advantageous, depending on your students and the situation. However, you need to consider every situation carefully. Your relationship with your students will help you make the decision as to when potentially risky techniques might be effective.

Circle of Influence

Attempting to create a low-threat environment at school doesn't even address the needs of those students who arrive already functioning in survival mode. Many children today are living in stressful environments. The economics of day-to-day living and the lack of emotional familial support are signs of our times. We see more and more children brought to school by siblings, just barely making it in time for the free breakfast program, not knowing where one parent lives and unsure about the other's job or income.

Children from more stable homes may also suffer from prolonged stress and anxiety. Over-scheduled children who have enrichment classes, lessons, or athletic practice almost every day can also feel helpless and fearful. The unreasonable demands on their lives may cause them to react reflexively rather than reflectively. Fixing what's going on outside of school may be outside your circle of influence. Some teachers do get involved with home visits and family support, but that is an unrealistic expectation for most of us. What we must focus on is what we *can* do in our classrooms, in our day-to-day contact with children.

Creating Schools as Safe Havens

The thought of rethinking *everything* about our school's campus and programs that would contribute to helping kids feel safe sounds overwhelming, impossible even. But creating an environment that is conducive to learning should be our first task, even before implementing the curriculum. It must be the foundation of everything that we do in schools.

The first key brain-compatible element is called *less stress*. This should describe the *tone* the school environment should have. It should be a place where harmony exists between the learner's brain and body, anxiety level, and curiosity. The climate must be one of low threat and high challenge. Such creative balance is the challenge for educators.

Finding Flow

Our first task is to acknowledge the profound effect that stress and threat have on the brain and body. As educators, we must first envision, and then create, environments that provide a low-threat climate. We must also investigate the elements that will maximize capabilities, promote positive behavior, and encourage students to be reflective. Just as we spend time on removing threatening stimuli, we must also consciously provide opportunities for students to experience joy, success, and satisfaction.

Psychologist and author Mihaly Csikszentmihalyi (1990) proposes an easy-to-understand suggestion in *Flow*. For 30 years, his team studied states of "optimal experience"; that is, times when people report feelings of deep concentration and enjoyment. He uses the term *flow* to describe a state of concentration that is so completely focused it amounts to absolute absorption in an activity. During a flow experience, the mind and body are in complete harmony. Self-consciousness, negative feelings, worries, and anxiety disappear. The activity takes on personal meaning, is intrinsically motivating, and results in total satisfaction.

Athletes reflect such flow when they refer to being "in the zone." Musicians and artists comment on having optimal flow experiences when they are deep in a creative mode or performing. You can apply the flow theory to any situation in which you are having or trying to create a positive enjoyable experience. Flow is the antidote for stress and threat! When one is deeply concentrating on a challenging task, the worries of everyday life are forgotten.

A central condition of flow is the balance between the challenge presented and the skills of the person to meet the challenge. If the experience challenges the student beyond what he feels capable of, he might feel anxious and respond reflexively. Conversely, if a student feels her skills are much greater than the task demands, she may become bored. Students are most likely to experience flow if the challenge is balanced with their self-perceived skills.

Teachers know they have orchestrated conditions for a flow experience when they look at the clock and announce, "Ladies and Gentlemen, we have run out of time today. Please start wrapping up your work and get ready to go . . ." and the response from the students is an immediate, "Ahhhhh, no! Can't we keep working on this? Do we have to stop? When can we do this again?" Isn't that what every teacher longs to hear? When activities in the classroom are learner-centered and students have had some choice and are working at an appropriate level of challenge, students get engaged! In order to provide opportunities to get into flow, teachers must adjust the daily schedule to allow for some chunks of time. Typical timelines in a self-contained classroom are often very predetermined and somewhat fragmented. Literacy blocks and students switching classes (or being pulled out frequently) don't encourage a teacher to plan for uninterrupted project or activity time. I recommend that teachers start requesting at least 90 minutes, two times a week, of "protected time." No interruptions allowed. No students gone to resource programs, and so on. Then, they can use these blocks to orchestrate tasks that encourage flow.

At middle and high schools, the concept of getting learners into flow is a terrific point to make when considering an alternative schedule. There are dozens of possibilities; I make one suggestion: Do the students have an opportunity at least two times a week to get into flow? Are the classes arranged in such a way that a teacher could orchestrate a hands-on lesson or project-based activity and encourage students to get "into it" for at least 90 minutes or more?

Csikszentmihalyi notes that there are eight major components of flow:

1. Flow occurs when we confront tasks we have a chance of completing.

2. We must be able to concentrate on what we are doing.

3. The task has clear goals.

4. The activity provides immediate feedback.

5. Deep but effortless involvement removes from our awareness the worries and frustrations of everyday life.

6. The experience is an enjoyable one that allows us to exercise a sense of control over our actions.

7. The concern for self disappears.

8. During a *flow* experience, the sense of time is altered; hours pass by in what seems like minutes.

Source: Adapted from Csikszentmihalyi, 1990.

Implications for Educators

As we begin to understand the overwhelming effects of stress, coercion, and threat on the human brain, we must look at traditional classroom discipline and management systems. The strategy many use to control a student's behavior must not also be the very thing that sets up another defensive reaction. We must shift our thinking to creating systems that promote optimal experiences. By designing instructional strategies and orchestrating systems that are based on flow theory and common sense, we can create truly brain-compatible learning environments.

In the 1990s, educators began to rethink the structures of schools and the way in which curriculum were designed and implemented. A big influence on the restructuring efforts was the results of brain research that were currently available. We knew that students could learn more if the curriculum was connected to their world outside school. We understood the importance of experiential learning and developmental stages. With greater understanding of the multiple intelligences, we were able to design a wide variety of instructional strategies and new assessment approaches. But even when our curricula are incredibly well designed and integrated thematically, if they are implemented in a brain-antagonistic setting, they are doomed to failure.

Since the enactment of No Child Left Behind (NCLB) in 2002, schools and educators have been in turmoil about the discrepancies between the results that the government is demanding by 2014 to be determined by state-level testing, and the implementation of appropriate, useful teaching strategies. We are in a difficult time. You need only peruse the top 15 articles on What Works Clearinghouse (http://ies.ed.gov/ncee/wwc/) to see that many of the successful models being presented do have various aspects of brain-compatible theory embedded within the programs. Another example worth downloading online is "Reducing Behavior Problems in the Elementary School Classroom" (Institute of Education Science, 2008) (http://ies.ed .gov/ncee/wwc/publications/practiceguides/index.asp#be_ pg). But sadly, brain-compatible teaching strategies haven't yet been credited for student success. It is incredibly difficult to document elements of brain-compatible strategies in longitudinal studies. So during this era of testing and Adequate Yearly Progress (AYP), the use of brain-compatible strategies must become part of a good teacher's tackle box of powerful tools, rather than just a suggested teaching model. Only a few schools have been willing to declare that their programs and teaching philosophy are based on brain research.

The strategies and activities outlined in this book can serve teachers, and their students, in important and relevant ways during the NCLB era. Understanding how to orchestrate a brain-compatible, learner-centered classroom will serve you and your students well in the current atmosphere of high-stakes testing. Many terrific teachers have felt coerced to set aside brain-compatible strategies to follow district and state guidelines that favor teaching to the test and often teaching to the middle. When we apply our understanding of how brains learn best in classrooms, students will benefit. Their abilities to learn will be enhanced and they will ultimately do well on tests. Courageous teachers will continue to teach with the brain in mind!

Is it possible to create an environment that has an absence of threat, as Leslie Hart (1998) suggests we shoot for? Given the wide variety of people, there really is no such thing as an absence of threat for everyone. The trick is to create a classroom and school environment in which the majority of students don't feel threatened but do feel greatly challenged. Mild stress and tension can actually promote arousal, and a curious emotional state will trigger engagement. This type of setting allows natural learning to take place. Joyful, rigorous learning should be our first goal. Creating schools that focus on simultaneously engaging the learner's intellect, emotions, creativity, and whole body must be the second goal.

I have developed the ideas I share here over the last 30 years as I have explored brain research and tried to integrate the new understandings into classroom practices. For veteran teachers, some of the ideas may be updated variations on some tried-and-true techniques, as well as an acknowledgment of the good things you are already doing. For newer teachers, suggestions at the end of each chapter give places to begin. While your intention may be to implement many brain-based strategies and learner-centered approaches eventually, your own brain can handle only so much new information before you yourself begin to have a reflexive response! I recommend using my motto: "I have every intention of doing it all, but I have the common sense to know that I can't do it all at once!"

WHERE TO BEGIN

1. I encourage you to expand your understanding of cognitive neuroscience. A terrific book to start off your investigation is: *Brain Rules: 12 Principles for Surviving and Thriving at Work, Home, and School* by John Medina (2008).

2. Whether or not you find time to read the following books from cover to cover, you will find them invaluable resources to your professional library:

Caine, R. N., Caine, G., McClintic, C., & Klimek, K. (2005). *12 brain/mind learning principles in action.* Thousand Oaks, CA: Corwin Press.

Jensen, E. (2005). *Teaching with the brain in mind* (2nd ed.). Alexandria, VA: Association for Supervision and Curriculum Development.

Sousa, D. A. (2005). *How the brain learns* (3rd ed.). Thousand Oaks, CA: Corwin Press.

Zull, J. E. (2002). *The art of changing the brain.* Sterling, VA: Stylus.

2

Welcome Home

Designing the Learning Environment

The learning environment must be orchestrated in a way that promotes a positive emotional climate as well as providing enriched complex experiences in a physically comfortable space. Research has confirmed that a stressful physical environment is linked to student failure, although low to moderate stress is not necessarily detrimental to successful learning. Many studies have confirmed that by paying attention to the physical details in the learning environment (lighting, temperature, color, air quality, seating, arrangement, and design), educators can enhance students' success. Research indicates that the brain responds to novelty and that there should be frequent changes in the décor.

Can We Do It?

First things first. Is it possible to create a classroom and school environment that might actually prevent stress and lessen threat? This kind of classroom would not be a source of confusion for children and would not induce a sense of anxiety or frustration. Wouldn't our time be well spent if we focused our energy on this kind of preventive strategy? Eric Jensen (2005), in *Teaching With the Brain in Mind,* reminds us, "Your ability to change the environment you work in has some limits. Focus on the greatest contributors to student success that are within your power to change. What you cannot influence let go" (p. 146). He suggests that to make the most of your physical environment, you should focus on

- Promoting feelings of a physically and emotionally safe environment,
- Incorporate opportunities for movement within the classroom,
- Monitor the room temperature and air quality, and
- Monitor the visual environment and acoustics.

Relaxed alertness is not the same as being calm and mellow. The goal is to create a climate that balances low threat with evidences of challenge for a wide range of students' interests and abilities. The environment must still have tasks, projects, displays, symbols, and clues that will instigate students' intrinsic motivation and attract their interest, attention, and curiosity. If they feel comfortable, then they will not put barriers up and therefore will be open to possibilities of reflection, attention, and engagement. When you achieve this balance of comfort, security, and stimulation, you have created a brain-compatible, learner-centered environment.

BEGIN WITH THE BRAIN BASICS

Attention: Filtering Out Sensory Input

To maintain sustained attention on a specific set of stimuli, the brain must orient focus while simultaneously suppressing irrelevant information being picked up by the senses. Students' brains are constantly bombarded with sensory input, which must be analyzed and evaluated. Where should attention be directed and what should be ignored? Several regions of the brain are involved in maintaining attention and vigilance.

Located in the core of the brain stem near the medulla, the reticular activating system (RAS) is the first gatekeeper and determines what information gets through to one's conscious mind. If the stimulus is perceived as a threat or a survival issue, it gets top priority. Can I eat it? Will it eat me? Can I mate with it? Have I seen it before? The

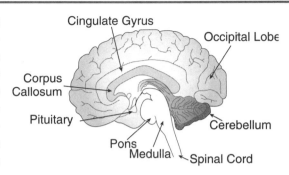

RAS maintains a state of alertness subconsciously and only brings information to our awareness if it is a possible threat, if it is useful to us right now, or if we have consciously preprogrammed a specific trigger to which we want to notice (baby crying, timer going off, etc.).

Factors that determine if the input will get past this primary filter include:

- Is it dangerous or a potential threat?
- Is it meaningful or useful?
- Is it unusual or novel?
- Is it humorous?

According to Mihaly Csikszentmihalyi (1990) in his book, *Flow: The Psychology of Optimal Experience,* we filter around 2 million bits of information per second down to seven (plus or minus two) chunks of information. In other words, in order for you to make sense of a situation and maintain attention, a huge amount of input is reduced down to a few key points. Maintaining attention (vigilance) can be a challenge as the RAS must always inhibit the majority of sensory input.

After information is identified by the RAS, it is passed on and processed in the emotional center of the brain (limbic area). The amygdala may trigger the *reflex response* if it perceives a potential threat. (See the Begin With the Brain Basics Box "Stress and Learning" in Chapter 1). If the sensory input stimulates our emotions and is determined to be interesting, valuable, or novel, it is passed on to the frontal lobes for higher-level processing. Now, the brain thoughtfully determines whether or not to make decisions or change behaviors.

The vigilance system within our brain helps us maintain attention by ignoring insignificant and irrelevant details. This system helps us filter out repetitive stimuli and things that aren't very important *right now.* Paying attention is more about ignoring stimulation than attending to it.

Research: *Educating the Human Brain* by Michael Posner and Mary Rothbart, American Psychological Association, 2007.

Practical Application: *Tools for Engagement* by Eric Jensen, Corwin Press, 2003.

Web Site: Brain Rules: http://www.brainrules.net/attention

Attending to elements in the physical environment is one of the core elements of *differentiated instruction.* By using formal and informal preassessments, teachers can get a clearer understanding of each student's skills, abilities, and interests. The instruction is designed, adapted, modified, or extended to best fit each learner's instructional needs. One aspect of differentiation is how a teacher might vary the physical environment in a way that supports and encourages each learner. Understanding which of the students are adversely affected by lighting or ambient noise, or who needs extra opportunities for movement, and so forth can help teachers consider how to arrange a classroom. For more research articles on classroom spaces, lighting, noise, and basic design, go to the Web site of the National Institute for Building Sciences and the National Clearinghouse for Educational Facilities (http://www.edfacilities.org/rl/design.cfm).

Sense of Security From Physical Harm

Carol Venolia (1988) writes:

> It seems obvious that we would not want to make buildings that harm our bodies—yet it's being done every day. Toxic materials, stressful lighting, unnerving noise, and unhealthy heating and air conditioning systems can all work against our well-being and are present, to varying degrees, in many contemporary buildings. (p. 64)

Schools across America have already had to address problems such as asbestos in the walls, formaldehyde under the flooring, and a variety of toxic chemicals used routinely in science and art classrooms. Research suggests that factors in addition to chemicals in today's classrooms may also do us physical harm, and we are only just beginning to understand their effects on our students and us. Yet, we do know that there is a connection between physical health and the ability of the brain to function at effective levels. To create truly brain-compatible classrooms, we must design body-compatible environments.

I was once interviewed by the local paper for an article to be published on National Teacher Day, celebrated at the beginning of each May. The reporter met me in my classroom after school. He commented that it seemed a little chilly, and I responded that the thermostat in my room had been broken for a while and we often were either too hot or too cold. He expressed shock! I then pointed out the sink that often backed up and wouldn't drain. He couldn't believe it! I told him that I had submitted appropriate work orders and that these issues would eventually be resolved, but that in the meantime the students and I had to try to work and learn in this body-incompatible environment. I decided that the main thrust of my "message" should be about how we as educators and the voting community need to create and maintain respectful, healthful, and safe learning environments for our students. Not quite what the reporter had expected!

In the first edition of this book, I introduced *The Healthy School Handbook*, edited by Norma L. Miller (1995), as an excellent resource for those interested in addressing environmental issues that may be affecting their students' health. The book cites comprehensive research done at Texas Woman's University that established 10 areas of major concern regarding maintaining ecological guidelines to ensure a healthful learning environment. They are listed here in order of their importance:

1. Heating, cooling, and ventilation, with proper mainte-nance being a top priority

2. Improper use of and overexposure to pesticides

3. Cleaning products that produce toxic fumes and irritate skin

4. Chemicals ranging from those used in copy machines to those in art and science labs

5. Fragrances such as perfumes and air fresheners

6. Sites near major highways, railroads, airports, television or radio stations, microwave towers, high-power electric lines, toxic dumps, or garbage incinerators

7. Lack of natural or full-spectrum lighting and inadequate lighting in classrooms

8. Installation of new floors, painting, roof repairs, and other remodeling

9. Floors that contain toxic substances and carpets that are not steam cleaned at least two times a year to remove allergens, dirt, and dust mites

10. Toxic art supplies or those not designed specifically for children; nontoxic art products are labeled "conforms to ASTM-D4236"

Another useful tool for teachers and administrators is put out (free of charge) by the U.S. Environmental Protection Agency. The *Healthy School Environmental Assessment Tool* (Healthy SEAT) (2007) is available online (http://www.epa .gov/schools/healthyseat) and provides an easy survey to determine how to improve the health of students and staff by ensuring that potential environmental and safety hazards in schools are being properly managed. Examples of school environmental hazards include chemical releases, pesticide exposures, flaking lead paint, mold and other indoor air quality problems, and damaged asbestos-containing building materials. All these areas and more deserve our attention.

The Basics: Lighting, Noise, and Air Quality

There can be negative effects on learners' bodies and brains from elements such as poor lighting, noise and acoustics, and air quality. Several studies on the effects of standard fluorescent lighting found in classrooms conclude that students' vision, fatigue levels, general health, posture, and concentration levels were negatively affected. In several studies, the flickering vibration of the fluorescent lights were linked to headaches, mild seizures, attention disorders, and hyperactivity. Based on a study done by the Illuminating Engineering Society of North America

(Bently, n.d.) in May 2000, the School and College Lighting Committee states that windows and daylight are indispensable parts of the learning environment. The report titled, "Recommended Practice on Lighting for Educational Facilities" says that exposure to daylight has shown to improve general health, mood, attention span, and behavior in the room's occupants.

Unfortunately, the standard classroom isn't designed with the brain in mind. In my classrooms, I try to cope with the lighting when I can by

- Keeping windows free from coverings and decorations and allowing daylight in;
- Turning off at least one row of the fluorescent lights and adding a couple of small lamps with incandescent bulbs around the room;
- Turning off lights when I read aloud to students or when using a data or overhead projector, showing a video, or using computers;
- Placing students who are affected by the lights in strategic locations;
- Providing colored overlays (yellow or pink) to use on pages with high contrast;
- Allowing some students with light sensitivity to wear a visor to shield their eyes; and
- Researching the possibilities of replacing fluorescent bulbs with full-spectrum bulbs.

Don't be hesitant to gather the research and provide a cost analysis to your school board and administration!

Our classrooms today are also filled with ambient noise, and students can't escape it. The light fixtures buzz, the heating and air conditioning system hums, and every new piece of technology has a cooling fan that runs. Even students with normal tolerance levels and attention spans complain of headaches and not being able to concentrate. Although we must be aware of how much noise and miscellaneous sounds our bodies are enduring, we can add some sounds that may soothe, heal, and mask the cacophony. A pleasant wind chime outside a window can add a comforting sound while making us aware of what is going on with the air outside. Quiet bird chirps can be relaxing and can come from a pet or a birdhouse or tree outside a window. Pet crickets chirping and frogs croaking can bring nature into the classroom.

Water is also a very soothing sound. I have visited many classrooms that have a small counter-sized fountain. You can purchase one at a department store or garden supply shop. I have also seen instructions for making a small gurgling fountain at landscaping supply stores and in magazines. Adjust the pump speed and arrangement of the rocks so that the sound is soothing and babbling. At first, it is not uncommon for students and the teacher alike to comment that the new water sounds increase their need to use the restrooms.

There are many CDs that have terrific environmental sounds. Gentle showers that turn into severe thunderstorms may not be as soothing as the steady sound of waves on a beach, so choose carefully. Forest sounds and evening crickets can actually make for a calming buffer against some of the everyday noises that we must endure from things such as lights, fans, heaters, projectors, and computers.

Good airflow and a constant room temperature of 68 to 72 degrees have been reported to enhance learning for most students. Many illnesses in children these days may be caused by the closed air systems that many schools have. Schools located near agricultural areas also must contend with toxic pesticides and fertilizers that are regularly applied to crops. Our responsibility as educators is to keep our students and us healthy. Watch for negligent practices, and be vigilant about creating healthful learning environments. Depending on the severity of the unhealthiness of the environment, you may want to begin to take stronger action. Seek support from other teachers, parents, and your principal. Begin to discover what would solve the problem.

Orchestrating a Harmonious Environment

Years ago, I was introduced to the work of innovative architect Carol Venolia (1988) and her book *Healing Environments*. Over the years, I have interpreted her thoughtful work into class-room design. Carol states, "Disharmonious environments can be sources of physical and mental stress" (10). So, any environment in which you are planning on spending time should include the key elements that promote health, relaxation, and positive emotional feelings. The environment should encourage interaction, be aesthetically pleasing, and above all else, do no physical harm. Great teachers have often designed their class-rooms intuitively knowing this.

If our goal is to promote student learning by maintaining an atmosphere of relaxed alertness, then we must evaluate the physical environment to see what elements might cause students to feel stressed, threatened, confused, or anxious. By doing so we can actually circumvent potential problems and work on prevention. Many refer to such evaluation of the environment as "front-end alignment" as we set the stage for powerful, successful learning. Whether you are trying to improve an existing classroom or design a new learning environment, and whether you are a veteran teacher or a first-time teacher, there are a variety of things to keep in mind. Venolia suggests some qualities we should strive to integrate to improve the healthful-ness of a place:

- Stimulation of positive awareness of ourselves and our students;
- Enhancement of our connections with nature, culture, and people;
- Allowance for privacy;
- Lack of possibility for physical harm;
- Meaningful, varying stimuli;
- Encouragement of times to relax;
- Balance of constancy and flexibility; and
- Beauty.

(Adapted from Venolia, 1988, p. 11)

I've taken these basic qualities, restated them in some cases, combined a few, then looked at ways a teacher may interpret these elements to design a brain-friendly learning environment.

Building Positive Awareness of Ourselves and Our Students

You can set up the classroom to reflect who you are and to reflect the qualities you like or want to encourage in yourself and your students. Include art you like and pictures of your own family, as well as any projects you are proud of that reflect a piece of you. As a reflection of who your students are, it makes sense to include pieces of students' lives, including class work, projects, art, and other things. Include pictures and other artifacts of students' lives, families, and interests outside of school. Also include evidence of their hopes, dreams, and potential. The goal is not necessarily to display it for others, but to display it as a reflection of the students themselves. What you shouldn't do is decorate the room for others: parents, teachers, observers, or the principal. Ask yourself, "What message does this environment send to my students?" The classroom should build students' positive awareness of themselves, what makes them happy and gives them hope.

Following are descriptions of ideas I have used successfully in my classrooms. While they focus primarily on students, remember that your classroom must also reflect you. Feel free to take part in the activities and displays yourself. Doing so shows your students that you value yourself as well as them, and that you don't regard the activities you ask them to take part in as beneath you. Many of the suggestions might seem more appropriate in an elementary classroom. I assure you that most of these strategies were modified and used successfully in my middle school and high school classrooms as well.

Displaying Students' Work

What is the most brain-compatible way to display students' individual work without the possibility of embarrassing, frustrating, or humiliating them? The obvious answer is to allow individual students to choose when and what they display. Public recognition of their efforts is something that some students have difficulty with and that others thrive on. Avoid a bulletin board or other area with a title like "Our Best Work" that has one of each student's recent spelling tests or all papers that got an A. Instead, call such an area "Our Personal Best." Each student selects something from the last week to put up for others to see and perhaps acknowledge. Occasionally, students might have nothing they care to share. It just wasn't a great week or they are working on a long-term project or product. Allow such students to pass on having their work displayed.

You could also allow students to create team bulletin boards. I have assigned a display area in the room to each table team. They are responsible for creating the display and presenting information. They have a certain time each week to meet and decide what will go up. They must include at least some of their work. Sometimes, they display only their team members' stuff. Other times, they organize and take one topic or product. For instance, Team B may decide to display the water quality graphs that we did in mixed teams. Team D may display the most recent limericks some students wanted to share. A necessary goal is to represent every student somewhere on the boards.

Place comment sheets next to the areas so that other students might write down positive thoughts and feelings about the work. You must first establish a degree of respect and trust among students for this to be successful. You must also ensure that students understand they are to write only positive comments.

Personal Posters

Allow students to create and display personal posters. You might have everyone participate at the beginning of the year, or you can assign one week to each student as a variation of the "Student of the Week" activity. Each student brings a few pictures from home—photographs of them when they were little, of family members, of pets, and of them doing things they like. They attach the photographs to a medium-sized poster with magazine cutouts of favorite stars, cars, toys, foods, and so on. As a variation, you might have a table team do their posters the same week and display them in their assigned classroom area.

You might choose to make the posters into graffiti boards. I provide small self-stick notes, and students write positive comments and compliments about the student and put them right on the poster. Again, you must establish a sense of mutual respect, trust, and guidelines first.

You could also make the poster assignment one of self-portraits and collages of favorites. Instead of photographs, students simply create a collage of all their favorite subjects in school, hobbies, sports, and other pastimes.

"Mirror, Mirror, on the Wall . . ."

Don't forget the obvious! What better item to have in a classroom that "reflects" positive self-awareness than a mirror. I've had large mirrors hung low enough for small children to see their whole bodies. In secondary school, I had a secret cabinet that had a 12-by-18–inch mirror inside the door. This secret mirror was so popular with everyone that I often had students who weren't even in my class stopping by between classes to sneak a peak and check hair, lipstick, clothes, and so on.

Real Things From Home

Students love to bring in personal items to share or just to have with them at school. Of course, sometimes it's necessary to make specific rules about the items. In self-contained classrooms, I often let students have an area of their desks or tables that they can use for displaying something special. Yes, I even let them tape pictures and things right onto the surface. It will be their responsibility later to remove them and clean the area. If your students have cubbies, consider allowing them to decorate the cubbies or have little creatures or action figures that live in there. Students bring in baseball cards, pictures of pop stars, stickers, skateboard decals, and even little Koosh creatures. Make sure you have clear guidelines to ensure that others don't mess with the items.

Don't forget that even high school kids like personal items with them. In secondary classrooms, I kept a basket for each team. I labeled the baskets according to the period and team, for example, "Period 1, Green Team" or "Table B, Third Period." Students keep Beanie Babies, stress balls, and so on in the baskets. They put the baskets on a shelf when their class time is over.

Your Stuff

Make sure that you have an area that reflects you and your interests. It can be a source of inspiration in the middle of a busy day. I always had photographs of my husband, kids, dog, and a picture of me at the age of the students in the class. I had little mementos that kids had given me. Several years ago, they started giving me things with apples on them or in the shape of apples. I would display this collection on a shelf near my desk. If you collect certain things, or support a particular sports team, display some of your items at school. One junior high teacher had a collection of *ugly* neckties. He hung them up on hooks under the chalkboard. He actually used them as hall passes for students when they had to leave during class time. They had to choose one and wear it as they walked in the halls.

Enhancement of Our Connections and Interactions With Nature, Cultures, and People

Just one hundred years ago, humans spent a large percentage of their waking hours outside. Even homemakers spent many hours outside doing laundry, gathering eggs, sowing seeds, making soap, traveling to town. Most of our lives are now dominated by indoor tasks and activities. Even when we go someplace, we simply pass through the outdoors on our way from a building to our cars!

Children spend *much* more time inside than children of previous generations ever did.

They simply aren't used to the outside environment. My neighborhood pals and I dug holes, built forts, picked berries, made street coasters, dammed up gutters, ate honeysuckle flowers, and watched clouds. Watching TV all afternoon was simply unacceptable! As a parent, I know how hard it is these days to encourage extended outside play, especially during hot or inclement weather when there are so many terrific diversions available inside.

As a result of our indoor society, we have a generation of children who are growing up without a solid understanding of what is just outside the front door. How can we expect children to engage in lessons and care about ecology and conservation if they haven't spent enough time outdoors to appreciate it? Likewise, if they haven't had a chance to connect and interact with other people and cultures in their own neighborhoods and cities, then they have missed a huge opportunity to learn about their peers and classmates. For many, basic understanding of other cultures comes from the media exposure they get, and there is a good chance that this exposure is biased and stereotypical.

Take the opportunity to create a microcosm of the student's real world. Collect items from nature and cultures in your community and school; display them in the classroom. Far better for children to see a basket of various seashells they can touch, smell, and feel than to never have a chance to see them at all! The following suggestions should provide some ideas for ways you can enhance such connections.

Plants

One easy way to create an enriched natural environment is to bring in a variety of plants. Several varieties are hardy enough to live under the fluorescent lights found in many classrooms: coleus, spider plants, ficus, and of course, many succulents and cacti. Hanging plants near windows can be a beautiful addition to a classroom. Or who can resist the sight of a bouquet of fresh-cut flowers? About once a month, I would stop by the farmer's market and pick up a bunch of colorful flowers and greenery. I tried to find the blooms that best represented the season. I encourage you to keep several inexpensive vases in various sizes in your classroom. As students see that you value the beauty of plants and flowers, they will start bringing you some from home, or small gift bouquets.

I know several teachers who opt for artificial plants in their rooms, especially if the plants are up high and far away from scrutiny or if they are in an area that simply can't support a live plant. But it always concerns me when teachers tell me that they can't get plants to stay alive in a classroom because the air is too dry or there's not enough sunlight. If plants can't stay alive in an environment, how can we expect children to thrive there?

Nature Brought Indoors

Designate an area of the classroom as a nature nook. You could use a table, a shelf, or a basket in which you and your students display artifacts from nature for investigation. Rotate the items regularly and encourage students to bring in things. Although this suggestion seems obviously appropriate for elementary classrooms, do not underestimate the power of it in secondary classrooms. Once in a while, the items will be things that will be ruined if touched: fragile butterfly wings, thorny thistles, or delicate spider webs. You can display those under glass or in some other way to keep them presentable. However, most of the items in the display should be *do-touch* items, such as the following:

- Seashells
- Birds' nests
- Driftwood
- Leaves
- Rocks
- Feathers
- Honeycomb
- Unusual vegetables
- Tree bark
- Sand and dirt
- Leather and fur
- Woven baskets
- Bamboo
- Various nuts

Expand the Learning Environment

We should also begin to see the learning environment as going beyond the four walls of the classroom. Is there at least some other space that you might develop at your school? A garden box or Life Lab gardening area is a wonderful place for each classroom to have a little patch of earth to try to grow something (see the Life Lab Science Program at http://www .lifelab.org). You can investigate creatures, dirt, and the effects of the weather. You can observe seasonal changes over time. Children who say they hate vegetables gobble up carrots, peas, celery, and broccoli when they grow and harvest the same vegetables with their own hands.

Some teachers have created small gardens in half-barrels and put them on wheels (available at garden supply stores). The minigardens can be wheeled inside at night if the weather is too harsh or security is an issue. Some classrooms have adopted a tree or planter box that already exists on the campus. They post a sign that indicates that the area has been "Adopted by Room 4" and take responsibility for watering, cleaning, weeding, and so on.

Some teachers have facilitated students' efforts to adopt an area near the school to clean and protect. A local creek bed, park, fountain, and highway can offer terrific opportunities for students to become responsible stewards. A key is to keep up the efforts for a whole year so that students can see the results of their efforts and to see what changes happen over time. You can study the cleanliness of an area, the growth, and the impact that humans have on your chosen place.

Bringing in People

Just as we expand our learning environment to include outside places, so we should consider expanding our exposure to other people in the community. Career days are a great way to introduce kids to the multitude of opportunities awaiting them.

You can also make regular visits to a local nursing home, a public library, a senior center, a preschool, a corner store, a hospital, and other businesses. Such field trips give children rich experiences with real people beyond the four walls of a classroom.

Celebrate Cultural Diversity

Every community of learners has a rich cultural background that should be showcased often through classroom projects and presentations. If there are celebrations or holidays observed in the community, consider allowing students, families, and other community members to share traditions and customs with the class. But I pass on a word of caution I received from Ventura Lopez-Cardona, a dynamic California administrator I had the pleasure of knowing. He encouraged teachers to be careful of trivializing cultures by celebrating only holidays. When we honor a culture only through its holidays, we tend to stereotype the people, traditions, and the celebration itself. Celebrating the influence of the Chinese in our community should go beyond learning about the Chinese New Year. Likewise, leprechauns and shamrocks don't really teach me anything about my Irish heritage.

Look for opportunities throughout the year for families to bring in heirlooms, pictures, and other artifacts. Share favorite family recipes, music, and games. Displaying evidence of the rich cultural heritage of our communities in the classrooms will help build an awareness of and respect for our community.

Private Places and Spaces

A classroom with anywhere from 15 to 35 students is one of the most difficult places to provide private spaces and places. Yet we know that humans have their need for control over the environment and crave at least some place that they can call their own, where they can be masters or mistresses of their domains. Adolescents also begin to feel territorial and seem to stake out areas of their own. In a middle school classroom, some dominant students may actually seem to mark their territory using what we may consider crude methods.

Having at least a semiprivate place for students to go for short periods of time can give them a chance to reflect, calm themselves, and regroup to build the energy it takes to interact with others. And according to Howard Gardner's (1983) multiple intelligence theory, students strong in intrapersonal intelligence will have a strong need to think, process, and problem solve in such privacy. It is imperative that we provide these students with a quiet, protected area and the time in which to process information and experiences.

Other students will use private places more as places for their things. In a traditional self-contained classroom with desks, students have a private place for their things that has some sense of security. For students who sit at tables or who are required to move among different work areas or classrooms, it will be important to provide places that are their personal space.

In classrooms that have team tables or other group seating, provide baskets, bins, or cubbies for students to keep their private things and works in progress. Cubbies should be at least large enough to fit a three-ring notebook, books, and a pencil box. I recommend that you provide plastic bins that can be pulled out of the cubbies like drawers to afford more privacy. These bins also keep little things from falling or rolling out. Students can also take the bins to their desks or work areas and then return them to the cubbies when they are through.

Portable Baskets or Packs

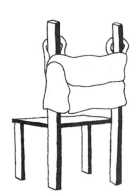

If cubbies aren't possible or practical, there are other ways to provide private, secure places for students' things. Some classrooms have plastic or cardboard book baskets that belong to the individual children and have their names on them. Students can set the baskets on top of their tables and transport them easily to other work areas. One year, my students made cloth packs that fit over the backs of their chairs. These were less bulky than regular backpacks, but still had a flap over the top to provide a private space for their books and other materials. These can be purchased now from educational supply vendors.

Reflection or Take-Five Zone

For students who are experiencing anxiety, stress, pressure, and emotional upsets, a chance to go outside, walk around or play, or go to the gym and exercise will help get rid of the pent up energy, restlessness, and frustration. For some students, a few minutes of quiet "down time," to get away from the source of stress and allow the individual a few moments of relaxation, will do wonders for his or her ability to stay calm and return to learning tasks. Providing a dedicated space within the classroom for this type of coping skill, and encouraging kids to notice signs of stress and take action, can be a powerful prevention strategy for students' positive behavior and success at school. There are several things that can disrupt the flow of learning and class participation of my students:

- Frustration about understanding and learning abilities;
- Anticipatory anxiety about upcoming tasks, tests, performances;

- Being overwhelmed regarding assignments, expectations, and even events going on outside of school (the over-scheduled child syndrome); or
- Worrying about a situation not related to school—a family member's illness or family problems; financial stress at home; and for older students, relationship issues.

Even the most meaningful curriculum and engaging instructional strategies often couldn't take students' minds off of these daunting real thoughts. Taking a few minutes for reflection is a very healthy routine to get into—not just for when you are getting overly stressed. I believe that it should be a basic human right to choose to take five minutes of calming time—with *no questions asked!*

I discovered that I could preempt many behavior problems and emotional upsets by designing coping strategies for the students to draw from when needed. In every one of my classrooms, I have created a "reflection corner," or more popularly known among students as "The take-five zone" (T5Z). Even in my smallest spaces, I would design a corner that had a special chair (rocking, bean bag, or just a padded seat), a few calming visuals such as photography books, mobiles, or the ever-popular lava lamp. This dedicated space might have "fidget toys" or calming stones to touch and possibly headphones with soft music. With clear standards and procedures for student usage, the space was available to all to visit for "five minutes with no questions asked." Students were encouraged to check their learning states and stress levels routinely. When too much pressure, anxiety, or looping thoughts started to derail the learning process, they were encouraged to take action and go take five or pause for the cause.

The Science of Reflection and Mindfulness

Allowing time to cool off or reflect on what's going on with your thoughts may seem like basic common sense, but research in the field of cognitive neuroscience has helped us understand that this reflection time is great for your brain and learning. Taking time to reflect on what is being learned and "thinking about thinking" are key strategies of metacognition. Taking time to reflect helps the brain make connections. Creating a neural network of connections helps us process the new information, relate it to our past experiences, and deepen our understanding. James Zull (2002) refers to this in his book, *The Art of Changing a Brain.* He points out that learners can be more successful in integrating new information if they can shut out other sensory information. "That way our brain is not distracted by receiving new information at the same time it is working with old information" (p. 167). Taking a few minutes for reflection when a student has hit *saturation* might provide a needed opportunity to let the learning sink in.

Sarah-Jayne Blakemore and Uta Frith (2005), cognitive neuroscientists and the authors of *The Learning Brain: Lessons for Education,* emphasize that "Stress is known to affect learning and productivity. Optimal learning occurs under a certain level of stress, but too much stress impairs learning" (pp. 158–159). They recommend using more visual imaging to help reduce stress. It is also noted that seeing some students learn how to deal with stress could promote others to imitate the strategy. The brain mirrors what it sees. Anytime one person in the class demonstrates how to manage his or her emotions, everyone benefits. Observing a disruptive student take five minutes to relax and de-stress could have positive effects on the whole classroom.

The most convincing research on mindfulness and relaxation training has been reported by Sharon Begley (2007) in her book, *Train Your Mind, Change Your Brain.* Begley documents how Dr. Richard Davidson, from the University of Wisconsin, convened a team of neuroscientists, the Dalai Lama, and a cadre of Buddhist monks to study the changes in the brain when practicing meditation and relaxation techniques. Through practice, studies confirmed, "happiness is something we can cultivate deliberately through mental training that affects the brain" (p. 229). The more one learns how to self-calm and change his or her negative thinking, the more the hard wiring in the brain adapts and reconnects, forming patterns for positive thoughts! Providing a space, encouraging students to monitor their negative thoughts and stress levels, and then teaching mindfulness techniques to relax are important life skills to give to your students.

Classroom T5Zs can be elaborate or simple, able to accommodate several or only one, quite separate from the classroom milieu or a simple chair off to the side. A few key design features should be considered.

Take-Five Zones

- A corner or separate area of the classroom, still within auditory and visual contact of the teacher
- A comfortable place to sit: a padded chair, a rocker, or large beanbag
- Pleasant visuals: an aquarium, a digital fish tank, a lava lamp, a photo or optical illusion book, plants or fresh flowers, a colorful wall hanging or poster
- Tactile comforts: hematite polished "calming" stones, quiet fidget toys, stress balls, stuffed animals, or Beanie Babies (depending on age of students)
- Auditory relaxation: nature sounds or quiet music on headphones, a countertop fountain, or noise-canceling headphones
- Timer: a visual tool to mark five minutes, such as a timer
- Water: a way for students to get a drink of water— paper cups and a dispenser

How the T5Z is introduced can influence how the students respond. I carefully review the importance of having a place to take five. I review the purpose and outline how it will honor their needs for a chance to

Take Five Zone

regroup and then rejoin the class. I design clear procedures for the expected behaviors for usage. I reiterate that if the zone isn't used for its intended purpose, then one would be asked to leave and return to an assigned seat.

It is possible that some students may not get the point of the T5Z at first. Others will be so grateful that a teacher is honoring their needs. Review the procedures and keep encouraging students to use the space in the way in which it was intended. After all, it's only five minutes! What have we got to lose? For an introverted student, an intrapersonal thinker, or a student who is simply having a rough day, this kind of refuge can make a difference in attitude and overall school experience.

Procedures for the T5Z

- Quietly go to the T5Z when you feel frustrated, overwhelmed, or upset.
- Set the timer for five minutes.
- Take a few deep breaths, and begin to relax.
- Use fidget toys, calming stones, and visuals to deepen your relaxation.
- Reflect on your current state, and feel compassion for yourself.
- Return to your seat when you are ready, after five minutes, or when another student is in need.

Forts and Hidey Places

There's nothing more inviting to younger students than a small hidey place that only a few of them can fit into at a time. Kids used to have more opportunities to build forts and tree houses in their own backyards. Many of today's children don't have an outside or inside place that they can go to for secret meetings or private, quiet times.

In your classroom, you can place a couple of cushions under a table. I once saw a classroom whose teacher had converted an old coatroom into a book nook. In primary classrooms, sometimes playhouses and puppet theaters can serve this purpose. Of course, as with any of these ideas, you need to establish appropriate times and procedures with your students.

Classroom Interactive Corner

Meaningful, Interactive, Engaging Stimuli

Sometimes, I will visit a classroom and there are so many decorations or student projects hanging from the walls and ceilings that I can hardly see the students! When our senses are overstimulated and we are bombarded with input, we may shut down in self-defense. But we can also get frustrated and bored with the monotony of a sterile environment. As Venolia (1988) states, "When we are exposed to unchanging temperature, lighting levels, noise, and sights, and when nothing around us moves or grows, our senses become dull and we function poorly" (p. 13). Place in the learning environment— including the classroom and hallways—a variety of hands-on, do-touch materials related to what the students are studying. Encourage students to bring in books, tapes, stuffed toys, and other items connected to the study theme. If the curriculum is relevant to them, you will be amazed at how much they start bringing in.

Bring in interesting puzzles, games, art supplies, and other items that will help students develop their skills. Provide stimuli that address a wide range of developmental abilities. You will be surprised at how older children will be attracted to some rather primary toys or games. These items don't necessarily have to relate to your current unit of study; they are important just for giving students a break or keeping them interested.

Encouragement of Times to Relax

If you can, provide physical spaces that promote relaxation, such as the T5Z mentioned earlier. You can also orchestrate certain times of the day or class time in which to encourage students to rest, relax, and experience calm.

As I note in Chapter 4, students also need opportunities to have fun! Do you plan playful times? Can you let yourself and your students get silly without feeling like you are losing control or respect? Parties and celebrations certainly help. Consider doing something playful daily.

You can often most easily help students relax by simply designating a time for silent reading, or "Drop everything and relax" (DEAR, which can also be an acronym for drop everything and read!). Students love it if during this quiet relaxing time they can sit on the floor or wherever they want. Although I originally set this time aside for reading, you may allow some students to do something else quietly, if they like; otherwise, they'll feel stressed instead of relaxed.

Anti-Coloring Books and Mad Libs

An excellent commercial product with which students have fun is Susan Striker's (1983a, 1983b, 1983c) *Anti-Coloring Book* series. The coloring books have simple, one-page activities that encourage creative thinking, inventiveness, and playfulness. Mad Libs are also a great tool for engaging the whole class in a game that teaches parts of speech, with a comical reading at the end of a session.

Balance of Constancy and Flexibility

Our brains and bodies will most likely feel uncomfortable if there is too much externally imposed rigidity or constant confusion and change. We must work to achieve a balance between things that students can count on to stay the same and elements that students can count on to change regularly.

When students arrive in the classroom, there should be a variety of things they can count on: daily agendas, weekly and monthly calendars, attendance and lunch management systems, procedures for exchanging assignments and homework, where to go for missed work, and so on. They will also begin to count on the ambience of a room. A particular design theme or color scheme could be your signature in a room. Warm lighting, curtains on windows, a welcome mat, soothing music, and a refreshing scent might be comforting signs students can count on.

At the end of one year, a fifth-grade boy told me he always liked coming in and smelling my perfume. I thanked him, but I told him I didn't think it was me. I had him investigate the room to see if he could find the source of the pleasant, subtle scent he described. He eventually found a lamp ring on a lamp on a back table. He commented that all year he had loved the peachy smell in our room and had just always assumed it had been me. (Before using an air freshener, scented oils, or potpourri, discover if any students have allergies. When experimenting, remember that a little goes a long way!)

It is also refreshing to enter a room and see changes from time to time. Decorations that reflect seasonal changes or thematic changes in the curriculum can be motivational and engage curiosity (see Chapter 6). A thoughtful change in the arrangement of the furniture or areas of the room can also give students a feeling of a fresh start or a new beginning.

Theme Corner

Have one area designated as a display area for the class's current theme unit, novel study, service project, or current events. While students may want the rest of the class to be constant, they will appreciate the frequent changes that might go on in this area.

Shifting Perspective

Occasionally, when I have needed to have a fresh start or to shake things up a bit, I have totally inverted the classroom perspective by turning the front of a classroom into the back. Sometimes, I moved my desk or a screen and overhead projector. It certainly helped get classes out of a rut. Involve students in proposing possible changes.

Beauty

As Venolia (1988) says, "The creation and experience of beauty is immediate, whole, and healing. It enlivens our senses, warms our hearts, relaxes us, and puts us at one with the entire surround" (p. 15). Even small touches of beauty enhance subliminal learning and feelings of well-being. Take time to bring beauty into the learning environment. Check out posters and art prints from school resource collections and public libraries to display in an area. Students will notice and admire objets d'art such as small statues, wall hangings, pottery, and sculpture, and they will appreciate your thoughtful additions to the classroom.

WHERE TO BEGIN

Of the many ideas suggested in this chapter, there are two I believe you should attend to no matter what!

1. Take time to observe the classroom from the perspective of the students. Sit at one of the desks and look around. What do you see? What distractions are there? What areas are too cluttered? Also check out lighting, noises, and air quality and take steps to improve them.

2. Select a classroom environment suggestion you can implement easily. Write a letter to parents asking for contributions. Your wish list can be broad or narrow. I send one of these wish lists home at the beginning of the year and at midyear. I am always amazed at the responses I get from families. Even parents who are struggling financially often send in a few items. On the last page of this chapter is a sample letter that could go home to parents.

Dear Families:

As your children's teacher this year, I will be trying hard to capture their attention, challenge them, and motivate them to be life-long learners. In my own research, I have discovered how important it is to create a pleasant and healthy learning environment. To make our classroom a comfortable place to learn, I am looking for some common items that you may be able to donate. If you can contribute or lend any of the following items, please call me at the number listed below. Thanks for supporting your children's school!

Healthy potted plants

Wall hooks to hang plants

Vases

Small area rugs

Welcome mat

Table lamps

Fish tank with pump

Lava lamp (do you still have one?)

Small baskets for materials

Sheer, café curtains and rods

Place mats (6–8 matching)

Large coffee mugs (for pencils)

Prints of art

Framed art

Small statues or sculptures

Sun catcher (hangs in window)

Suction hooks (for glass)

A framed wall mirror

A small candy bowl or jar

Seasonal flags or banners

Small wall clock

Extension cord

Sincerely,

Martha Kaufeldt

3

Meeting Students' Basic Needs

Building the Foundation for Learning

Basic physical and psychological needs must be satisfied in order for the brain to be able to focus on complex tasks. The brain's first job is to maintain survival by meeting the basic physical needs of food, water, sleep, and shelter. If the brain detects a physical need, the reflex response will take over until that need is met. Is it any surprise, then, that poor learning has been linked to children's being hungry, tired, thirsty, and physically uncomfortable?

Basic Human Needs

As we begin to address the importance of setting up a brain-compatible learning environment, we must also consider how students strive to get their basic needs met. From the field of psychology, two models have emerged to describe the fundamental drive that humans have to survive. Introduced over

60 years ago, Abraham Maslow, a student of classical Adlerian psychology, developed the hierarchy of basic needs describing humans' instinctual drive to survive. At the very basic level all of us require air, water, food, rest, activity, to get rid of wastes, to avoid pain, and eventually seek out a mate and reproduce. If these basic needs are not adequately met, then we are *driven* to get them satisfied.

In 1986, William Glasser wrote *Control Theory in the Classroom*. He described how he believes that "we always choose to do what is most satisfying to us at the time . . . Control theory is about payoff, what we need as human beings to be satisfied" (p. 19). What we *choose* to do is always our best attempt *at the time* to feel satisfied. This theory is opposite of the stimulus-response theory that states what we *do* can be motivated by the people and events going on outside of us. Glasser refined his theory and modified the title of his ideas in his 1998 book, *Choice Theory, A New Psychology of Personal Freedom*. Glasser describes that in addition to meeting our basic need to stay alive, grow, and reproduce he also believes that

- We need to feel *love and to belong,*
- We need to experience control and feel *powerful,*
- We need to feel as if we have choices and have *freedom,* and
- We need to feel pleasure so we seek out *fun.* (Adapted from Glasser, 1998)

When it comes right down to it, I can categorize almost all student behaviors I observe in the classroom according to these five *needs.* Whether it is Cody, the class clown, doing something silly to get us all to laugh and lighten up or Danielle's constant need to be with a partner and to feel included. Getting one's basic needs met is a strong survival response. Learning will always take a back seat when the brain is first and foremost trying to feel *satisfied.*

Physiological Needs

The first needs we must satisfy are physical. We must find ways to eat and drink to avoid hunger and thirst, and eventually, to ensure survival of our species, we must find ways to reproduce. We must also relieve ourselves. Many elementary students' basic hunger is not satisfied, not to mention their nutritional needs. But school is about efficiency and economy, and the idea of allowing students to eat, drink, or go to the restroom whenever they "need to" seems difficult to implement or, to many, even counterproductive. However, these needs are overwhelming and biological; students cannot help but seek to meet them. They often act in ways that we deem inappropriate because they are actually hungry or thirsty or because they have to use the restroom.

Instead of helping them meet these needs, we come up with complex reward systems to try to control their behavior. Such attempts, as Kathy Checkley (1998) noted, are counterproductive: "When teachers offer students rewards, they ask them 'to forget their needs'" (p. 6); in other words, we ask them to place gaining the rewards above their own biological needs. Checkley goes on, "Kids can do that for a while, but not for the long term" (p. 6). We teachers must realize that if we can orchestrate a way that students can satisfy these needs, then we will prevent other problems. We will also have far more time to spend on actually teaching and learning instead of striving to implement a reward system that works against students' best interests and drives.

Thirst and Dehydration

The effects of thirst and dehydration on learning have been widely researched. Carla Hannaford (2005) discusses it, as does

Eric Jensen (2005). Not only is mild dehydration linked to poor learning, but it also appears to contribute to stress levels. If some of your students' diets are salt laden, they may crave more fluids than their peers. If they drink a lot of soft drinks, coffee, or other caffeine-laden drinks to quench their thirst, then their bodies are actually in worse shape because caffeine is a diuretic. When the human body is not adequately hydrated, the brain tells it to fulfill the need. The response to being thirsty is very clear-cut: find water, now! The problem can be complicated by the fact that children often don't realize that, in fact, their headache or general discomfort is a result of thirst or even dehydration. They may not know what to ask for to feel satisfied; they just know they are uncomfortable.

How much water should kids drink each day? This is a simple question with no easy answers. Studies have produced varying recommendations over the years. An individual's water needs depends on many factors, including where you live, the weather, how much exercise you do, and what kinds of foods you have been eating. The FDA and other nutritional experts recommend that we all drink a lot of water, although all fluids count toward the daily totals. While not supported by hard scientific evidence, it has been recommended that young children should drink at least five eight-ounce glasses a day and teenagers and adults should drink at least six eight-ounce glasses. Another recommendation is to intake one ounce of water for every two pounds of body weight. Encourage your students to drink water throughout the day. They can drink other fluids as well, such as juice and caffeine-free sodas, but the most essential beverage for good health is water.

Here is an easy solution for keeping up one's daily water intake:

- Drink a glass of water with each meal (3 × a day)
- Drink a glass of water between each meal (2 × a day)
- Drink a glass of water before and after exercising

You might see barriers to allowing students to drink more water. What if students ask to leave the room to get drinks all of the time? If they drink a lot of water, then won't they have to use the restroom, too? Can't they take care of this at lunch and breaks?

I got over these concerns in first grade. I had recurring bladder infections, and the doctor told my mother to write a note to my teacher asking her to allow me to drink plenty of water and use the restroom as I needed. I remember the teacher announcing to the *whole* class that I was going to have this special privilege and get to drink water *whenever* I wanted to. I'll never forget the look on all of the children's faces every time I got up to go get a drink. It seemed as though they were very uncomfortable, thirsty, and jealous of my special status. Their looks made me want to find a way to sneak water back into the class! I knew in my heart, even at that age, that keeping children from satisfying their basic need for water was fundamentally wrong.

Free Drinks

As long as you have classroom procedures that include getting a drink whenever a student needs one, then you shouldn't have problems with allowing it. Of course, it is more convenient if you have a sink or drinking fountain right in your classroom. One element of the procedure you'll want to include is that students not interrupt direct instruction or a student presentation. Good manners dictate that they wait until the speaker is finished. However, if they are coughing, choking, or totally distracted by their thirst, encourage them to make a quick, nondisruptive jaunt to the faucet.

Bottled Water

Have plastic water jugs filled with purified spring water (not distilled). If you have a source to help fund water delivery, try to get your hands on even the five-gallon dispenser. Most often, it is an inexpensive, two-and-a-half gallon jug with a spigot that sits on the counter by the sink. I've actually had various parents donate one jug per week. I used to ask students to bring in plastic mugs with names on them and have set up hooks with their

names written on labels in an effort to be less wasteful. Unless the classroom has access to a dishwasher for frequent washings, this isn't the best solution for maintaining a healthy classroom. Now, I provide children with paper cups with their names on them at the beginning of the day; they throw the cups away at the end of each day. Not a particularly green practice, but practical when we are dealing with a classroom of students.

Some teachers ask students to bring in their own individual water bottles or reusable sports bottles; they keep the bottles filled at their desks. It is important that students take these home each day for cleaning or recycling. Common sense tells us that refilling plastic bottles without thoroughly cleaning them might promote bacteria growth and illnesses. It has also been reported that the integrity of the plastic in the bottle is not designed for refilling and might breakdown with washing and reuse. (Caution: Many secondary schools do not allow water bottles or sports bottles from home. Some teenagers have filled the bottles with liquids other than water!)

The W.O.W. Method

A school nurse that I once met had developed the W.O.W. strategy for dealing with students sent to the office with headaches and not feeling well or feeling tired. I have had great success sharing this strategy.

W = Get a drink of fresh *water*. Go to the bathroom if you need to.

O = Get a few deep breaths of fresh *oxygen*. Stand by an open window or door for a few minutes.

W = *Wait* five minutes. Take five to rest and relax.

Often, students ask to go to the office or see the nurse for minor symptoms. With a drink of water, a breath of fresh air, and a few minutes to regroup, I've observed that up to 90% of the students are willing and ready to return to their classrooms.

BEGIN WITH THE BRAIN BASICS

Eat, Drink, Sleep . . . Repeat

The brain is wired to maintain homeostasis. Hungry, thirsty, and tired brains will set aside opportunities to learn, seeking out food, water, and rest in order to feel satisfied and calm. The brain stem controls basic functions that are critical to survival: breathing, heart rate, sleep, digestion, and reflexive movements. A little higher up is the hypothalamus. This region controls additional basic processes important for life: hunger, thirst, body temperature, daily sleep cycles, and sexual behavior.

Nutritionally speaking, what's good for your body is good for your brain. What you eat, how much you eat, and when you eat influences your brain's ability to function. Glucose is the brain's fuel; using up to 20% of the energy needed by the whole body. Very low glucose levels can weaken our ability to concentrate, remember, and pay attention. Here are some general guidelines for a brain-friendly diet:

- Complex carbohydrates break down into glucose at a slow rate to keep the brain supplied with adequate energy. Fiber rich foods, such as whole grains and vegetables like broccoli, are converted into a slow and steady dose of glucose.
- Small amounts of low-fat protein rich foods such as dairy, eggs, and nuts (especially in the morning) are broken down into amino acids that help the brain create neurotransmitters associated with attention and memory.
- "Good" fats are especially important. Foods rich in omega-3 fats, such as fish and olive oil, are linked to healthier brains that seem to have more resilient memories.
- Iron in the diet plays a key role in helping the blood transport oxygen to the brain.
- Antioxidants are nutrients, found in many fruits and vegetables, that can improve brain function and health. Blueberries are a great source.

Many studies have linked mild dehydration to minimized brain functions. Water plays a vital role in metabolic functions. It is estimated that 80% of the brain is water and that even a drop in hydration of 2% can cause fatigue and short-term memory loss. Maintaining adequate water intake may help with brain function and promotes production of neurotransmitters such as serotonin and melatonin. A common guideline for daily water intake is one ounce for every two pounds of body weight. The amount of water consumed should be increased with exercise and if the weather is hot.

A variety of experiments have shown that different stages of sleep can improve learning. Lack of sleep may interfere with attention and the acquisition of new learning. Studies show that periods of REM sleep may enhance learning consolidation. Research suggests that it is during sleep that synaptic pruning may be taking place. Neuronal firing has been documented during REM sleep, indicating that the brain may be replaying important activities and learning that occurred during the day. This improves the synaptic connections and enhances memory of the important stuff.

Research: *Keep Your Brain Young* by Guy McKhann, MD, and Marilyn Albert, PhD, Dana Press, 2002.

Practical Application: *Learning and the Brain* edited by Sheryl Feinstein, Rowman & Littlefield, 2007.

Web Site: Water for Wellness: http://www.waterforwellness.us/healthy_hydration.html

Hunger and Malnutrition

It is equally important to meet children's need for food, and those needs are not always met. Despite the millions of dollars in free and reduced-cost breakfasts and lunches, some kids still go hungry. Children are smaller than adults, and their stomachs are smaller. They usually simply cannot consume enough food at one meal to provide the calories they need to get them all the way through to the next. Nor should we want them to. Repeated studies show that children are more likely to overeat and become overweight if we force them to eat on a schedule rather than in response to feelings of true hunger. Also, when children go through growth spurts, they may feel famished most of the time.

At Monarch Community School, a large population of students qualified for free breakfast; however, to receive it, students had to be at school at least 30 to 45 minutes before school started. A great many of their parents didn't get them to school in time for it, for whatever reason. Kids who showed up late went to class with no food in their stomachs. The free breakfast was either packed up until the next day or thrown out if it had been prepared fresh. What a mixed-up system! I'm happy to say that, after a great deal of lobbying, we were able to serve an additional "cold" free breakfast during morning break. Many more students were able to get what they needed, which helped create an environment in which they were more likely to perform well.

If students say they are hungry, don't assume they are trying to get out of doing the work at hand. Instead, find ways to have available in your classroom some nutritious snacks that aren't messy to eat. Remember that young children can't always articulate their hunger needs; they often say, "I'm tired," or, "I don't feel good." I usually don't even wait for a student to ask for a snack. As I get to know my students, I can often tell when they seem to have low blood sugar or lack energy. They always seem so relieved when I point out that they may be hungry. Understand that many teenagers will seem to be hungry all the time because their bodies go through so many changes during these years. I provide snacks for them, and I also give them ideas about what things they can bring in their own backpacks to help satisfy them throughout the day.

Snack Cupboard

If possible, keep a variety of healthful snacks in a cupboard. Individually wrapped items, although ecologically wasteful, help with portion control and cleanliness. Generic granola bars, trail mix, fruit snacks, and crackers are  always the most popular items. When reasonable, ask parents to donate these items. I would actually tell the parents of the children who hit the cupboard most often. They would send in a box of graham crackers now and then and express their appreciation for the opportunity to contribute.

Bathroom Breaks

I believe that students shouldn't have to ask to relieve themselves. I know many schools and classrooms must adhere to rather rigid school rules regarding when students can go to the bathroom. If you implement proper procedures, including the ideal times to take breaks if they can wait, ways to do so without disturbing others, and so on, then students can simply answer the call of nature without it creating conflicts.

In a multiage fourth- through sixth-grade class, we had a single unisex bathroom in the classroom itself. Students used it much like we use the bathrooms at home—whenever they needed to go. Of course, there were occasions when students went in to work on their hair, and one student who always took a book to read while he took his time doing his business. I dealt with these problems individually; I did eventually limit their bathroom use. I recommend that you, too, make stricter standards for the few who abuse the right rather than impose rigid rules on everyone.

Potty Passes

If your school has rigid break rules, then create potty passes that allow two students at a time to leave your classroom. I always asked students to put name cards in a pocket by the door so I knew who had left the room and where they were. You might offer students brief bathroom breaks every hour to ensure that students know they can relieve themselves when they have to.

Psychological Needs: Belonging, Fun, Freedom, Power

Even when students' physical needs are met, they still may not be ready to learn. In his earlier book, Glasser (1986) refers to belonging, fun, freedom, and power as essential psychological needs that drive us all. He notes,

> The more students can fulfill their needs in your academic classes, the more they will apply themselves to what is to be learned. . . . No class can ever be satisfying unless both teachers and students find it so." (pp. 30–31)

It is quite easy to make your class satisfying in the way Glasser means.

Belonging

To belong to a group and feel included and cared for is an important need. If your students never have the opportunity to disclose information about themselves, their families, their likes and dislikes, and their concerns, then they perhaps feel judged only by their outward appearances or behaviors. They can become obsessed with these two elements of themselves rather than focusing on the parts of them that truly make up who they are. Develop procedures that help students share themselves with one another; such opportunities will ensure that they get to know more about the others in the class and recognize things that they may have in common. It will help them focus on the parts of themselves that are real and important rather than just on how they look. Chapter 5 offers many ways to address this need to belong and feel important and cared for by outlining ways for students to belong to many different groups within a classroom.

Fun

Fun and joy are closely tied to learning. The best teachers are those who can turn learning into joyful, enjoyable experiences. Monotonous tasks don't cut it. If the learning environment gives students opportunities to play, laugh, and experience joy, then students whose need for fun is greatest (class clowns!) will have times each day to satisfy their needs.

In 2003, a team of researchers at Stanford University confirmed that a good joke activated the reward circuits in the brain that release dopamine (Pearson, 2003). Research shows that laughter can lower stress and perhaps even triggers the immune system to help fend off disease. A good laugh also improves memory and attention (Jensen, 2005). Do you give your students the learning gift of at least one good laugh each day?

A Joke a Day

Assign students different days to share jokes with the class. This assignment opens up great discussions about boundaries, appropriateness, and respect. You might need to screen younger children's jokes. It is also easy to sign up for an online joke service. One of the most ridiculous and most visited sites on the Internet, and yet great fun, is the Light Bulb joke Web page (http://www

.lightbulbjokes.com). You can even get kids motivated about the Internet by asking them to search for jokes! If you can't really handle a joke a day, how about a joke a week?

Theme Dress-Up Days

During class meetings or as part of an entertainment committee, students can plan a theme dress-up day. Just for fun, they select a day and dress up. Some great themes include pajama day, baby day, weird hat day, crazy hair day, and grown-up day. For even more fun, involve the whole school. Give certificates as awards for participation and prizes for the kids who are really into it. Make the days even more hilarious by getting adults involved in the fun, too. You may feel that such days are likely to distract students, but that hasn't been my experience. Of course, you'll have to allow a little more time at the beginning of the day for the laughter and frivolity. If students have decided to award prizes, do that ceremony by the morning break so students who want to take off their costumes can do it.

Music and Dance

There's nothing like a chicken dance or hokey pokey to bring out the silliness and clowns in a classroom. Such dances promote fun movement and playful singing. I've even taught the hustle (an old disco dance for those of you too young to remember), the electric slide, and a little stomp dance that has West Indian roots! Bring these gems out at various times to loosen things up and get people moving and laughing.

Freedom

Freedom, another basic need, seems almost the opposite of belonging, and to some degree, the opposite of power, as well. Even though we may seek out competition and desperately want to be included as part of a group, we also want the freedom to choose when, with whom, and for how long. The right to choose is a powerful freedom. We can observe people become quite nasty and reactive when they feel that their choices will be limited or lost altogether. I rarely get to experience it these days, but I love it when I can say that I have some "free time" next week. To me, this means I have the freedom to do what I want to do, to fulfill some of my wishes, goals, and needs. My time isn't scheduled to meet anyone else's needs; I will have the freedom to choose, and I will experience a strong sense of satisfaction in that. When I have the freedom to choose, I don't always choose frivolous or recreational activities. I might actually feel like I have the time to begin a work project I'd been postponing.

Classroom freedom doesn't necessarily result in chaos. Students will positively respond to a time each day, or during a class period, when they have the freedom to choose what activity they work on, what they read during silent reading, or what center they sign up for. If they complete their work, do students have freedom to choose what to do while others are finishing? By giving children a chance to be self-directed, you will be giving them a chance to experience and learn self-control. Chapter 8 offers many activities that give students choices.

Power

The need for a sense of power over our environment, others, or ourselves is particularly difficult to satisfy, especially if you are a kid. In fact, we all almost always compete for power. Motivated individuals are ambitious and might worry about "winning." The list of how we worry about power is endless: our need to be right, to be recognized, to achieve, to influence others, to look good, and so on. Even those people whom you know are not driven by power and are quite humble sometimes compete for who can be the most humble!

Some students feel powerless in their home environment, in situations with friends, and at school. They may push hard to have this need fulfilled. The more you can give them a sense of control over themselves, the more you can help them see what is in their power, the more self-directed they become in their learning. Chapters 7 and 8 outline many ways to grant students power over areas of classroom management.

Learned Helplessness

When students have repeated experiences feeling helpless, or feel that others are controlling their activities and actions, they may begin to show signs of *learned helplessness.* Lack of power begins to program the learner to only focus on what others want them to do. They begin to have difficulty understanding what to do next and rarely take initiative or set their own goals. Simply put, the more teachers and parents do for children, the less likely they might be to actually begin to try things for themselves.

Martin Seligman at the University of Pennsylvania developed the concept of *learned helplessness* in the 1970s: "Human motivation to initiate responses is also undermined by a lack of control over one's surroundings" (*Encyclopedia of Childhood and Adolescence,* 2005–2006). The Caines (2005) describe learned helplessness as the *opposite* of being in a state of relaxed alertness (p. 24). Anxiety, depression and low self-esteem begin to emerge as the individual begins to blame himself for everything. Children who fail repeatedly in school will eventually stop trying if they don't see how they can do something to be successful. If students are always told what to do, they won't develop the skills needed to discover what needs to be done next, where to go, what materials are needed, and so forth. They often sit and wait for someone to tell them exactly what to do.

In classrooms, I have observed well-intentioned teachers streamlining tasks for students and in some cases actually redoing and finishing activities to (in their minds) help children be successful! This holds true for younger students as teachers manage students' materials, schedule their daily activities, tell them when to eat, go to the bathroom, and so on. Older students show signs of learned helplessness after years of having caring teachers orchestrate their school experience to such a degree that they never have had an opportunity to be in charge of their own learning!

Giving a student a jump-start or helping them over a hurdle to get on to the next stage of learning should occur as a teacher determines. But I encourage you to reflect on your daily interactions with students.

Don't Do for Students What They Can and
Should Be Doing for Themselves!

Our intentions are good, but research and observation shows that when we don't allow students to develop initiative and problem-solving, they become dependent on others to guide them and miss out on opportunities to learn.

WHERE TO BEGIN

1. Find out what your school rules are regarding eating food and drinking water in classrooms. Some schools have strict rules about these issues. If your school is one, then decide at least to develop a way that allows students to get drinks of water when they need them. If you have more leeway, then follow one of the suggestions for getting water and snacks in your classroom. Send a note home to parents about your snack and drink philosophy and procedures.

2. Over the next two weeks, observe your students, ask them questions, and find other ways to collect data about their physical needs. Is there a certain time of day that many of them seem to fall apart? What kinds of breakfasts, if any, are they having? When do they eat when they get home? What healthy snacks do they like? Do only a few need snacks and water, or do they all need such sustenance? Consider sending a note home to parents asking them to donate such snacks.

3. Plan something fun with the students, such as Crazy Hair Day or Twin Day! Get into the spirit yourself!

4

Routines and Procedures

Organizing Systems for Orderliness

The brain innately seeks to detect familiar and useful patterns in its environment. These patterns give a context to what otherwise might be interpreted as meaningless. These meaningful patterns, when practiced, become wired in the brain as programs and routines. The brain seeks to make order out of chaos. It organizes and associates new information according to previous experiences or similar circumstances. You can establish patterns of appropriate behavior and systems for doing things in a classroom. These logical patterns create an organizational strategy for dealing with each type of event or experience that comes up in a classroom. Confusion and frustration will be reduced, as the brain feels secure in knowing and detecting the pattern for appropriate behavior.

Your Assumptions Drive Your Classroom Systems

When students arrive in your classroom, they will notice *you* first, get the feel of the environment second, and then begin to scan the room for clues as to how the place runs. Older students may be looking for classmates and peers whom they know. Younger children are interested in what centers, displays, and toys are out. And everyone wants to know where they will sit!

How the systems within the classroom are set up will reflect your basic beliefs about children's behavior. Alfie Kohn (2006) asks teachers to consider their own assumptions about the motivation behind what children do. Reflect on the following statements. They are often at the heart of more traditional class-room management systems.

- Do you think kids are always trying to get away with something?
- Do you believe that children should be told exactly what to do and what will happen to them if they don't do what they are told?
- Do you believe that you should give positive reinforcement to children who do something good or nice if you want them to keep acting that way?
- Do you feel that children need to be taught self-restraint to control their impulses?
- Do you believe that children are driven by wanting power, control, or superiority?

- Do you believe that children need to feel pain or loss before they will stop behaving badly?
- Do you feel that you can identify troublemakers early on?
- Do you believe that if you give kids an inch, they'll take a mile?
- Do you assume that teachers must get and maintain control of the classroom; otherwise there will be chaos?
- Do you believe that children are basically untrustworthy, selfish, or aggressive?

When we look at results of brain research, developmental stages of children, and the new information regarding emotions and how we process them (Gazzaniga, 2008; LeDoux, 1996, 2002; Posner & Rothbart, 2007), then our views about children, their capabilities, and their needs begin to shift. As Kohn (2006) notes,

> Teachers who assume that children are capable of acting virtuously can likewise set into motion a self-fulfilling prophecy. They can create an "auspicious" circle rather than the more familiar vicious one. Thus, if a teacher trusts her students to make decisions, they will act very differently from those in her colleague's classroom if left on their own; typically, they will act responsibly and go right on with their learning. (pp. 7–8)

As educators develop a more positive view of children and their motivations, the real-world impact will be powerful. We must begin to consider what things we need to put in place for children to flourish instead of considering how we can make them do what we want.

The Office of Special Education Program (OSEP) Center at the U.S. Department of Education has developed a successful model referred to as the Schoolwide Positive Behavioral Support (SWPBS) program. The SWPBS model is described not as "a curriculum, intervention, or practice, but [it is] a decision-making framework that guides selection, integration, and implementation of the best evidence-based academic and behavioral practices for improving important academic and behavior outcomes for all students" (PBIS, 2009, para. 1). This process for developing a schoolwide proactive behavior model moves away from traditional punishment and disciplinary systems and can be adapted to any school. The focus is on

(Continued)

(Continued)

> prevention and teaching and supporting kids regarding positive behavior patterns. To see how this process is being implemented in many schools, visit the Web site: http://www.pbis.org (Positive Behavior Interventions & Support)

Classroom Standards and Courtesies

Positively framed prevention strategies are the key here. By establishing, teaching, and rehearsing expected standards and procedures, teachers provide knowledge and experience with examples of the appropriate responses and behaviors for situations students create and encounter in the classroom. First and foremost, you should create a brief list of your basic standards and expectations. The list is not one of rules because they are stated *positively*. You don't post consequences by the list; students understand that everyone in the classroom will always attempt to meet these basic standards of behavior.

Many classrooms keep their standards simple: "Demonstrate Respect and Responsibility to Yourself, Others, and the Environment." When you think about it, that simple statement really covers everything!

DEMONSTRATE RESPECT AND RESPONSIBILITY TO YOURSELF, OTHERS, AND THE ENVIRONMENT

In 1986, Robert Ellingsen, an exceptional classroom teacher, a friend, and at that time a fellow associate of Susan Kovalik, put together what he referred to as "Rules to Live by." He felt strongly that classroom standards should reflect ways responsible adults are expected to behave in the real world. Consequently, he included no "Do Not Do" rules or trivial things; that is, he had no rules such as "Do not chew gum" or "Use only white paper for written assignments." Based somewhat on the *Tribes* (Gibbs, 1995) standards (see Chapter 5),

Ellingsen's "Rules to Live by" proved very effective at a variety of grade levels and were ultimately refined and incorporated into Susan Kovalik's integrated thematic instruction model as "Lifelong Guidelines." Later, Robert and I taught together for four years at Monarch Community School, and the classroom standards evolved into the standards in Figure 4.1.

Figure 4.1

Monarch Community School Classroom Standards and Expectations

- Be trustworthy and truthful to others at all times.
- Be active listeners; use your ears, eyes, and heart.
- Show respect to others by giving up Put-Downs.
- Show respect to yourself by always doing your personal best.

So, why a list of standards instead of rules? A classroom rules list does not prevent misbehavior; in fact, rules seem to invite it! Rules were meant to be broken! In Robert DiGiulio's (1995) *Positive Classroom Management,* he states that rules and laws may be necessary in huge societies but inappropriate in the small, more personalized world of a classroom. By associating punishments with broken rules, we teach students that they can trade misbehavior for a short, meaningless time-out or other such consequence. Such a system sets up the escalating endless spiral. As DiGiulio notes, "The only thing the teacher can do in response is to raise the stakes by making the punishment increasingly distasteful in the hope that fewer will opt for it" (p. 16).

DiGiulio goes on to point out that "rules can transform any clever student into a 'classroom lawyer,' engaging the teacher in arguments over the meaning of classroom or school rules" (pp. 26–29). He offers a list similar to Ellingsen's classroom standards called "Four Basic Understandings" (see Figure 4.2).

Figure 4.2

Basic Understandings That Encourage Prosocial Behavior

1. Respect is nonnegotiable
2. Cooperation over competition
3. Achievement is valued
4. Full inclusion is practiced

(Adapted from DiGiulio, 1995)

After establishing standards of behavior, we must discuss with our students what "common courtesy" means. Students of any age can participate in such a discussion. With the discussion comes understanding of the premise that we must honor and respect others until they demonstrate that they are not worthy of our respect. We know students have varied experiences. Many children have not had respectful or courteous role models; they may not even have had opportunities to observe such behavior. In general, you and your students may list some of the courtesies listed in Figure 4.3.

Figure 4.3

In general, we can describe courtesies as

- Words and actions that regard and treat other people humanely.
- Signs and indication of consideration for others.
- Words that communicate feelings of remorse when we make a mistake.

You must teach courtesies concretely, by modeling them and practicing them within the classroom. Such a theme makes for terrific role-play opportunities as students generate possible scenarios.

Ms. Manners

Role-play social situations that give your students practice with courteous language. First, brainstorm courteous words and phrases on the board. Then, write down several social situations in which someone would have to be courteous: getting in line or getting on a bus, asking someone for an empty chair, accidentally bumping into someone at a store, accidentally spilling something on a stranger. Choose one of the situations at random and ask students to illustrate it. Then pair them off to act out the scene and insert as many of the courteous phrases as possible. Try to be over the top on how polite you might act. (We used to call this "Eddie Haskell" because students would try to be as overly sweet and sickeningly courteous as the character on the old *Leave It to Beaver* show. I'm afraid that now few students are familiar with this classic archetype!)

Creating Classroom Management Patterns

 BEGIN WITH THE BRAIN BASICS

Patterns and Programs

To make sense of and organize the vast amount of information it's expected to process, the brain creates patterns. Beginning in infancy, through observation, repetition, and trial and error, children sort information into recognizable and memorable patterns, determining how things work. With multisensory experiences, neurons wire together into neural networks. Recent brain research indicates that these programmed responses might actually be whole columns of nerve dendrites that fire in a pattern when triggered.

Cognitive neuroscientists believe that our brains develop "schemas" or "templates" (patterns of specific cognitive processes) when we have interactive experiences with the environment. These templates are what we draw on when exposed to new information. They are the unique patterns in our brains of how we have learned something. Most learning appears to be a process of fitting new information into old schemas. The brain needs immediate feedback to determine if the selected schema is appropriate. The brain often has to do a trial and error approach to see what works and what doesn't.

The brain is an incredible pattern-seeking instrument, constantly trying to find some order in our chaotic world. Leslie Hart (1998) emphasizes the brain's propensity for searching the environment for cues and clues to make sense of an experience. When the brain notices a symbol, an action, or something it has a memory of and prior experience with, then it begins to implement a program it has stored that will be an efficient, and hopefully appropriate, response. A program can be described as a series of related actions that can be triggered and to which one does not have to consciously attend, much like a line of dominoes that fall in a quick, almost unstoppable system when the first one is pushed. When triggered, programs can be implemented unconsciously. This allows us to be able to do two (or more) tasks at the same time. We count on them to make our lives easier throughout the day. We rely on a stored program to wash up in the shower while we consciously are thinking of the 101 things we must do.

Acquiring patterns and developing useful programs builds a learner's ability to quickly connect new learning to prior experiences. Confidence and motivation grows when one can rapidly determine a recognizable pattern and detect the appropriate program to implement.

Research: A User's Guide to the Brain by John J. Ratey, MD, Vintage Books, 2002.

Practical Application: Your Brain: The Missing Manual by Matthew MacDonald, Pogue Press, 2008.

Web Site: Dana Foundation: http://www.dana.org/news/cerebrum/detail.aspx?id=2320

We must understand a little about how the brain stores the information and later how it would select that set of procedures to use. Leslie Hart (1998) referred to this process as "the program implementation cycle" (p. 158). About this cycle, he states that, "We select the most appropriate program from those stored in the brain to deal with what is happening at the time" (p. 158). He notes some apparent steps the brain takes in implementing a program (see Figure 4.4).

Figure 4.4

How the Brain Uses Procedures

- **Evaluate**: You must reasonably and accurately evaluate the situation or need (detect and identify the pattern or patterns in the environment); otherwise, you simply do not know what the problem or task is.
- **Select:** You can choose and select only from those patterns and programs with which you are already familiar and already possess. If there is no frame of reference from which to draw, then you do not know what action will be appropriate. You simply do not know what to do.
- **Implement:** You cannot implement a program unless given a chance to do so. If the implementation isn't a total success, then after feedback, you must have another chance to select and implement a different, perhaps appropriate, program (p. 158).

When you have a chance to utilize an evaluate-select-implement system, and you have a great many that work well, your confidence in implementing such programs and in yourself rises.

Creating simple procedures for the classroom, teaching them, and giving students chances to implement them gives students a set of familiar programs that they can use as a part of their go-to system when they approach classroom tasks. The goal is to create routines by teaching and allowing students to practice their own programs. When students evaluate activities, select the appropriate procedures, and implement them automatically (that is, without prompting or supervision), then you know that the procedure is a habit or a stored program in their brains.

Designing Procedures

Harry Wong and Rosemary Tripi Wong (2009) note that "the number one problem in the classroom is not discipline: it is the lack of procedures and routines" (p. 165). Procedures can be a method, process, or a set of expected behaviors for how things are to be done in the classroom. They allow students to learn, be successful, and to function effectively. Teachers must take responsibility to make the learning environment safe and secure. By creating standards, patterns, and procedures, they can better ensure that there will be minimal ambiguity, frustration, or confusion for the students. With a little forethought, you can outline the most basic classroom procedures and create systems that will be simple to implement. Later, with the students' help, you can create additional procedures as the need arises. The list of procedures is your go-to system that helps your students know what default behavior they should at least try in certain situations.

Most often, when a teacher has asked me to observe and give feedback on a classroom lesson, the most common problems are related to procedures and processes, not the content of the lesson itself. When a teacher says something as seemingly benign as "Okay, class, hand in your work," students will respond in a variety of ways. Some may start shouting things out: "Wait, I'm not done!" "Can we turn it in after lunch?" "Do I have to copy it over?" "What should we do if it's not here?" Other students might move. John immediately starts walking toward the teacher, paper in hand. Emily gets up and starts collecting other students' papers, grabbing some from their desks, provoking angry reactions. Jason immediately gets out of his seat and goes over to Dylan's table to copy the last answers onto his own paper. Marcus uses the teacher's distraction by all this as an opportunity to run to the back and get a drink of water and take a quick look out the window. What should have been a simple request with an organized, respectful response can become a few moments of chaos and a huge waste of time.

If the teacher had established a procedure for turning in papers, introduced it on the first day of class, modeled it, and asked students to rehearse it until it became routine, the chaos and confusion might have been avoided entirely. Figure 4.5 illustrates a possible procedure for the preceding scenario.

Figure 4.5

Procedures for Handing in Work at the Same Time

- Hand in whatever amount you have completed at the time.
- If you don't have it at all, put your name on a blank paper with the title of the missing assignment and the date, and hand it in. Do this if you were absent when the assignment was given.

(Continued)

Figure 4.5 (Continued)

- Write concerns or questions at the top of the work.
- Stay seated, and quietly pass the work to your table leaders.
- Table leaders organize the papers, put them in the team folder, and place it in the file at the back counter.

Well-designed procedures for various activities allow for several different activities to be going on at the same time, which is imperative if you are orchestrating differentiated instructional strategies or learning environments that encourage choice, movement, centers, and so on. Procedures can also help ensure that transitions take place efficiently, with a minimum of wasted time and confusion. No procedure will work, however, if you don't take time to teach it to students and give them opportunities to apply their understanding of the procedure. We want students to know how to assess each situation in the classroom and, in essence, to choose the correct set of behaviors for the activity.

Wong and Wong (2009) contend that there are a few reasons why students do not follow procedures. The main reason is that they do not know the specific procedure for a particular task. They perhaps have not had a discussion or an opportunity to personalize the procedure; that is, they have not been trained to follow the procedures by practicing and role-playing. Most importantly, I have found that teachers have not really thought through what happens in the classroom and taken time to create procedures for the basic activities.

Pat Belvel and Maya Jordan (2003) draw a distinction between procedures and instructions: "Classroom procedures clearly define and establish the *social* parameters for specific activities, distinct from directions, which establish the *task-related* parameters of a specific activity" (p. 112). I have used Belvel's recommendation to develop the procedures in Figure 4.6.

Figure 4.6

Well-Designed Procedures Should

- Be unique to each type of activity;
- Describe, clearly define, and positively phrase social behaviors needed for the specific activity;

- Include behaviors that can be observed;
- Involve students in their formulation;
- Be reviewed prior to the activity;
- Help maintain consistency; and
- Provide students with a sense of security

In a classroom, there are a wide variety of tasks, activities, and transitions that demand that you design procedures. Think through what behaviors you expect your students to follow in each situation:

- Morning arrival
- Class moving to another location
- Transitions within the classroom
- Gatherings and class meetings
- Student seating
- Independent work time
- Collaborative group work activities
- Going to lunch or break
- Movement of materials and papers
- Use of supplies
- Getting teacher help
- Student classroom jobs
- Use of restrooms
- Quieting a class—getting their attention
- Silent reading or work time
- Dismissal

Write procedures as briefly as possible, in positive language. If you find that you have more than five or six steps in a procedure, you might want to reexamine it to determine if you have actually combined two procedures. For example, you may have a procedure for silent reading after lunch that includes steps for entering the room, quieting down, getting a book, and finding a place to read. You actually have the steps for entering the room and getting settled in with the procedure for silent reading, and you will want to separate the two. One question to ask yourself is, "Are these steps all exclusive to this activity, or will there be other times when I want students to follow some of them?" The following questions can be answered within the steps of procedures:

- How do I want students to work together?
- How do I want students to work independently?
- How do I want students to communicate? (Silently? In 12-inch voices? Not at all?)
- How do I want students to use their time while on a task or at a center?
- How do I want students to use their time when they are finished with a task (anchor activity, free choice, or reading)?
- How do I want students to situate themselves (individual seats or small groups)?
- How do I want students to use or get materials they need?
- How do I want students to get help from other students or me?

The following is a collection of procedures for a variety of activities. You can use them as they are, alter them to meet your needs, or throw them out completely and design your own from scratch. I mean them to serve only as guidelines. I developed some myself, and some were procedures the Monarch Community School developed to implement schoolwide.

Reading Circle or Literature Response Group

- Bring pencil, learning log, and book
- Sit in designated seat

- Put date on new page in log
- Use whisper voice to practice vocabulary and spelling words

Direct Instruction

- Active listening; no talking
- Raise hand to participate or share an idea
- Stay put

Morning Routine (Primary)

- Greet teacher and one another
- Take off jacket, and empty backpack
- Sign in on attendance chart
- Place lunch bag in basket or lunch card in pocket
- Go to morning choice center

Completed Math Work

- Put completed work in basket
- Choose math activity from list
- Begin activity immediately
- Work alone

DEAR Time (Drop Everything And Read)

- Get book or reading materials (approved list only)
- Sit where you wish (no counters, cupboards, or closet)
- Rotate groups for rockers and beanbag chairs (check schedule)

Getting Teacher Help

- Ask three, before me
- Find something you *can* work on while you wait
- Put name on "Help, please" list
- Come to me if in a panic

Monarch Coed Bathroom Procedures

- Door stays closed when not in use
- Knock twice and wait for response
- Respond with "Uno Momento!"
- Boys: Lift seat, *please!*
- Wash and dry hands
- Wipe off sink
- Leave everything *clean and ready for next person*

Monarch Outside Play Procedures

- Bounce balls against big wall only
- Stay in fenced area
- Throw balls only, not rocks and dirt
- Walk around and up the ramps
- Climb on structures only, not railings
- Respect our beautiful trees! Climb on the base of the big tree only!

When writing up procedures, I try to always start each directive with a process verb. This makes the statement an imperative, a command. I often highlight the verb with color, underline, or all capitals. I try to state the procedural tasks in positive language to help students see what they are supposed to be doing as opposed to emphasizing what they are *not* to be doing. "Keep your eyes on your own papers" is much more productive than "Do *not* look over at another student's paper!"

Make PB and J

To give students practice in writing steps before involving them in writing classroom procedures, ask them to write out the steps for making a peanut butter and jelly sandwich. To make it even more fun, ask one pair of students to do a presentation to the class. One student is the director and sits in a place where she cannot see the sandwich maker. The sandwich maker stands in front of the class with all the ingredients and must do only what the director says. If the director says, for example, to get the peanut butter out of the jar and spread it on the bread, the sandwich maker must use his hands because he wasn't told to pick up a knife first. This game really helps students figure out that procedure steps must be clear and complete. Younger children can draw the steps in an illustrated flowchart.

Brainstorming Rules

Older children love collaborating on a group list of *all* the miscellaneous classroom rules they have had over the years. You will probably be amazed at what things they remember. This activity will most likely take some time, but when they are done, students will have a huge list that you can ask them to categorize. From these categories, work as a class to write general rules or standards that can encompass all of the little rules. I've actually had students narrow the list until the only thing they said needed to be posted as a standard was "Show respect." It really does cover it all, doesn't it?

WHERE TO BEGIN

1. If you do not already have a set of classroom standards, use the statement on page 78, "Demonstrate Respect and Responsibility to Yourself, Others, and the Environment." Post it for the first day of school. Later, you and your class can modify the statement or develop your own classroom standards.

2. Decide what area most necessitates a set of procedures ready to go. Depending on the age of your students, you may want to develop procedures for some basic, everyday activities: arriving, dismissing, talking, getting materials, getting help, going to restrooms, getting drinks, and so on. Use the sample procedures on pages 86–87 to get started. Add some of the graphics shown on page 90 (next page) to make the list of procedures more appealing.

Graphic Symbols for Procedures

5

Building Community and Managing Conflicts

Orchestrating Positive Social Interactions

The brain's capabilities are enhanced by positive social interactions. One's own identity and the ability to learn are profoundly influenced by noncompetitive, interpersonal relationships and one's feelings of inclusion in a social group. A safe and secure emotional climate that promotes strategies for resolving conflicts is a key to successful learning. When you organize collaboration opportunities properly, you give individual learners a great asset. When we work cooperatively with a group toward a common goal, our brain releases neurotransmitters that are related to pleasure and enjoyment. The brain also responds to immediate feedback. When interacting with others, the group provides feedback so that students can evaluate their own ideas and behaviors and begin to modify them as necessary. By actively processing experiences with others, learners can internalize information in personally meaningful and coherent ways. With time and repeated interactions, the groups will eventually build emotional connections and a sense of community.

BEGIN WITH THE BRAIN BASICS

Our Social and Emotional Brains

Neuroimaging technology such as an fMRI (functional Magnetic Resonance Imaging) can reveal to researchers our thoughts, moods, and thinking processes. Scientists can literally see different areas of the brain "light up" when people are asked to recall a joke or think of something unpleasant. While all areas of the brain are interconnected, specific regions have been identified with certain behaviors and processes. Many areas of the human brain are similar in structure to animal brains, but there are a few key regions that are uniquely human and contribute to our ability to connect socially and emotionally with others.

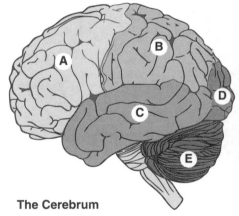

The cerebral cortex and is divided into two hemispheres. We can think of the cortex as a quadrant: The back three lobes (occipital, temporal, parietal) *receive and analyze* sensory input and create a perceptual map of the current situation. The frontal lobes *develop and execute responses* to challenges and powers our conscious thought. The right hemisphere focuses on *novel challenges* that require a creative solution. The left hemisphere focuses on *familiar* challenges that can be answered

The Cerebrum

A – Frontal Lobe   D – Occipital Lobe
B – Parietal Lobe   E – The Cerebellum
C – Temporal Lobe

by an established response. The cortex thus analyses and responds to novel and familiar challenges from our space-time environment.

- **Frontal Lobe**—Complex integrated brain functions: thinking, planning, conscious understanding of emotions, inhibiting impulses. Includes the prefrontal cortex "Executive Brain"—the area most unique to the human brain.
- **Parietal Lobe**—Saddled across the top of the head, plans and controls movement, orientation, calculation, and some recognition.

- **Temporal Lobe**—Located above the ear, processes sound and speech comprehension (left side), some memory.
- **Occipital Lobe**—At the back of the cerebrum, primarily visual processing.
- **Cerebellum**—"Little brain" tucked in the back under the cerebrum, coordinates balance and movement.
- **Brain Stem**—Sitting on top of the spine, filters input and controls body functions.
- **Mid-Brain**—Limbic area, includes the amygdala—the emotional center—hippocampus—the memory center—and the thalamus—the sensory center.

Developmentally, the brain matures from the bottom to the top, from the back to the front, and from the right to the left. The prefrontal lobes are the last to mature during adolescence—which may not occur until the late 20s.

To assure human survival, specialized areas of the brain have developed. Social intelligence is defined as the ability to understand others and respond appropriately in human relations. Many brain areas are involved when we interact with others. Young brains need to learn how to communicate appropriately with others, form emotional bonds, and develop strategies for working and problem solving within a group.

Scientists have recently discovered clusters of neurons in the premotor cortex (between the parietal and frontal lobes) that fire off when we plan and initiate a movement. These same neurons also fire off when we *see* someone else perform a similar movement. These *mirror neurons* may help us to predict someone's intentions and allow us to build empathy for others as we understand and "feel" their feelings.

Research: *Mirroring People: The New Science of How We Connect With Others* by Marco Iacoboni, Farrar, Straus and Giroux, 2008.

Practical Application: *How the Brain Influences Behavior* by David Sousa, Corwin Press, 2009.

Web Site: Nova Science: http://www.pbs.org/wgbh/nova/sciencenow/3204/01.html

Welcome Aboard

Just as a host and hostess create a first impression when they greet and welcome you into their home, you will create a first impression of the learning environment when you greet your students. Our looks, words, attitude, constancy, knowledge, self-respect, and authority will influence how students regard the rest of the room and the tasks at hand. We are the human connection to the learning environment.

It is important to be friendly and encourage students. Be sure to stand near the entrance as they come in. Smile and make eye contact with all students as they enter the room. A handshake or a hand on the shoulder or arm will immediately break the ice and make your first connection. As Harry Wong and Rosemary Tripi Wong (2005) note, "When significant people use significant words and actions, they increase the likelihood of receiving positive behaviors from other people" (p. 76). Wong and Wong also note that the effective teacher does the following:

- Addresses people by their names and pronounces the names correctly
- Says, "Please" and "Thank you"
- Has a controlled, disarming smile
- Is lovable and capable (p. 77)

Teacher Relationships

When teachers take the time to establish themselves as capable, respectful, friendly, and joyful, students will be more likely to trust them, engage, and respond positively in the classroom. In his book *The Art and Science of Teaching*, Robert Marzano (2007) cites dozens of studies confirming that "the quality of the relationships teachers have with students is the keystone of effective management and perhaps even the entirety of teaching" (p. 149). There are two main elements that must be conveyed by the teacher to the students:

- You can count on me for clear direction about your behavior and learning.
- I care about the success of each one of you, and we are a team!

Teachers need to establish and maintain behaviors that students recognize they can count on as well as demonstrate daily that they *care* about students. This might include the following ideas:

- Getting to know something about each student: his or her family, interests, activities, friends, gifts, and talents. Interject this information into conversations.

- Setting up a routine for greeting students and getting class started: welcoming each student by name and making eye contact, engaging in friendly conversation, demonstrating a passion for learning and an "I'm excited about what we are doing today!" attitude.
- Piquing students' curiosity and reducing stress and anticipatory anxiety with agendas and creative class beginnings (see Chapter 6).
- Being consistent in maintaining rules, procedures, expectations, and consequences.
- Maintaining physical behaviors that communicate joyfulness, caring, encouragement, and concern: smiles, eye contact, pats on the back, high-fives, or "fist bumps." (Fist bumps, also known as fist pound, knuckle knock, givin' props—as in giving or getting "proper" respect—and various other regional names, have been a great way to show respect and congratulations to someone on a job well-done. What seems to have evolved from the high five, sports figures, rap artists, and celebrities routinely use this greeting and acknowledgement with each other. Walk over and offer up a fist bump to a middle school student for a great answer and you will generate an immediate smile and begin to make a great connection!)
- Keep your own negative or frustrated emotions in check, and try to keep a consistent, positive tone in the classroom. Avoid glaring at students, raising your voice or yelling, finger pointing, and really watch how you use sarcasm . . .

Teaching Prosocial Behaviors

For the last 25 years, every educational reform movement, restructuring document, standards guide, or new curriculum strategy has recognized and included the recommendation that students have opportunities to learn prosocial behaviors. It is obvious that our survival depends upon our young people's capacity for cooperation, interdependence, conservation, and respect for others. It's been said that the "Me" generation may well be recognizing the need to help create a "We" generation. Many educators believe that the ability to work in groups, participate in democratic planning, and maintain caring social support groups and communities will be the key to success in the 21st century. By experiencing and learning group participation and communication skills early on, our young people will be able to develop into resilient, caring, cooperative adults. The research also shows that academic achievement will improve as the teaching strategies include more collaborative learning experiences within a caring community of learners.

What is a "community of learners?" Alfie Kohn (1999, 2006) believes it is a place in which students feel cared about and are encouraged to care about one another. They are able to experience a sense of being valued and respected. They feel connected to one another and the teacher, and most importantly, they feel physically and emotionally safe. In an inclusive classroom, students see that they are helping the group towards a common good—the good of others in addition to their own individual good. They learn how to get along with one another and how to be part of a group. They learn how to get their needs met, but not at the expense of others. Successful learning and heightened, realistic self-esteem strongly support providing opportunities for students to work in a variety of groups and collaborate on processes, products, decisions, and tasks. As Jeanne Gibbs (2006)

notes, "The system of long-term membership in the Tribes process assures support for all members within each small group and within the classroom. This *intentionally created environment* supports development and achievement for students of all abilities" (p. 70). Such benefits are the result of any intentionally created group system.

> Jeanne Gibbs (2006) started the Tribes program nearly thirty-five years ago. Many educators recognize it as an exemplary educational program. Tribes defines its primary mission as "to assure the healthy and whole development of every child so that each has the knowledge, skills and resiliency to be successful in a rapidly changing world" (p. 10). The Tribes process requires that a group stay together for an entire year: "A major difference between Tribes and some of the other classroom group methods is that people maintain membership in the same group for an extended period of time. This is based on research indicating that people perform better on learning tasks when they are members of 'high cohesion' rather than 'low cohesion' groups; and students who feel comfortable with their peers utilize their academic abilities more fully than those who do not" (p. 69).

A wide variety of grouping strategies for the classroom exists. Flexible grouping is a key component in a learner-centered classroom emphasizing differentiated instruction. Children can and should see themselves as members of multiple circles. Teachers might organize minigroups according to student interest, ability, projects, research, or social alliances.

Multiple Student Connections Within the Classroom for Various Tasks

Your goal is to create a brain-compatible environment, a place that promotes positive interactions while keeping students from minimizing their capabilities by having to deal with fear, threat, and frustration. If students feel included in a classroom and see themselves as part of multiple support groups, they immediately feel a sense of security and empathy. They can also draw energy, ask for feedback, and receive encouragement from a partner or a group of peers when they feel overwhelmed.

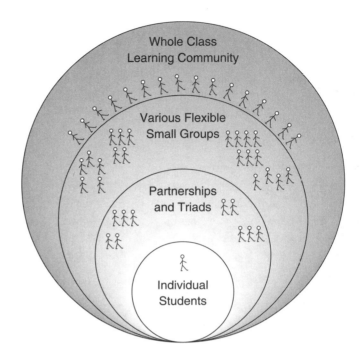

Designing *cooperative learning* opportunities for students to work together on tasks and projects is a valuable teaching tool and a chance for students to develop interpersonal skills. Looking at the bigger picture, teachers who take time to nurture a classroom *community of learners*, the reward is even greater. Orchestrating systems for group development and for community building takes a little time, but it has a great payoff for your students and you. Taking part in a variety of groups can be a major portion of the learning interactions throughout the day, or in the beginning you may make a decision to use the groups for only certain situations. Understanding the various types of groups can give you choices as to how you might implement them.

Building Relationships, Inclusion, and Belonging

To orchestrate successful group experiences, you must have a basic understanding of the stages groups go through as they begin to form, bond, and create a sense of community. By designing standards for group communication, you will keep the interactions safe and productive. Consider the following suggestions and see where you might implement more group experiences.

Most of the cooperative learning models or community building programs use the term *inclusion* to describe the first step or stage that a group must experience to be successful. Groups must then establish agreements and develop process skills. As time progresses and group members have opportunities to work on tasks and solve problems together, a community spirit and sense of caring develop among the members.

Learning to accept and trust one another in a group can occur only when the following occur.

- All members feel they have individual opportunities to introduce themselves and share their interests, talents, feelings, and concerns.
- All members can express their individual opinions, hopes, and goals without being interrupted.
- The group welcomes and appreciates all participants as valuable members.
- All members see similarities between themselves and the others in the group.
- All members value the group's diversity.

You should regularly orchestrate specific activities that encourage students to build relationships and create a sense of belonging. Select activities that are appropriate for the age level, interests, and length of time your students have been together. Students young and old often need a prompt or gimmick to start sharing. You might begin with simple-response questions such as the following:

- What's your favorite restaurant food?
- What's something you like to fix for yourself?
- What's a good movie you've seen recently?
- What kind of car would you like to have if money were no object?
- Where would you like to go for a vacation?
- Where in town do you like to go for fun?
- What is your favorite store?

Four Corners

Label each corner in the classroom as either A, B, C, D or North, South, East, West or Red, Blue, Yellow, Green. Provide a possible response to a prompt you are about to give. Students get up and stand in the corner that best suits their own response. Consider one of the questions stated above. "Where would you like to go for a vacation?" Each corner might be labeled: (A) a beach resort, (B) Disney World, (C) an African safari, or (D) camping. Students make a forced decision and choose one response that best describes what they want. By going to that corner, others are able to learn something about them. Students are able to begin to see which classmates are like-minded. This response strategy has many variations as an instructional tool, and it also supports movement and socializing—two things the brain needs regularly to feel satisfied and engaged.

Adapted from Kagan, M., Kagan, L., & Kagan, S., 1999.

Eventually, you can ask questions that generate more thoughtful responses:

- If I were an animal I'd be a _____ because . . .
- When I'm older I want to . . .
- The last time a really felt sad was when . . .
- A thing I would like to change about is . . .

The goal is to give students opportunities to share a variety of things about themselves. When they must reflect and consider their responses, it builds a greater understanding of themselves. By sharing about their preferences, thoughts, and opinions, and listening to others, participants will begin to see similarities and feel connections. Only when group participants begin to feel as though they are a part of a group will they start to exercise their powers of persuasion, influence, and compromise.

Developing Group Processing Skills and Making Agreements

This stage of building groups involves learning strategies that will encourage members to express diverse opinions and personal feelings without feeling judged, as well as developing basic processing skills. During this stage, the group will learn effective group communication skills, various problem-solving strategies, simple and fair decision-making models, conflict resolution and compromise methods, steps for planning and organizing, and strategies for sharing leadership. Agreeing how and when the group will work together is also appropriate for older students.

To build such processing skills, the group must have multiple opportunities to talk about and wrestle with tough ideas. Robert Slavin (1994) states that students should practice cooperative learning by working in pairs or small groups at least 50% of their day to ensure success. Presenting them with a real-world problem or working on a simulation can give students a chance to plan as a group. When groups work together, the members naturally begin to demonstrate and practice negotiating and compromising skills. Following is a list of possible small-group discussions or tasks:

- The group brainstorms, discusses, chooses, and plans a special event in which the whole class will participate.
- The group discusses how much computer or video game time students the members' age should be allowed on a school night, and then makes a group recommendation.
- The group comes up with a new system for checking out balls during recess.
- The group discusses and comes up with three suggestions for ways that surplus crops from local fields might be distributed to area residents.

With time, groups who have opportunities to build relationships, work through adversity, make decisions, set goals, and experience success become ready to function truly as a team or community.

Building a Caring Community

You'll find that your students' groups begin to demonstrate heart-felt interdependence and connection among their members. The members feel dedicated to resolving problems. The group practices skills that enable collaboration. The community celebrates its successes. This collective confidence is a wonderful thing to observe in students. To maintain the community spirit, they must build relationships through continued work and collaboration. When new people are asked to join a group, the group must begin at the first stage again to make the new member feel included.

I have seen groups who have reached a remarkable level of caring. I remember a fifth-grade girl who was experiencing an extreme family situation. As a result, she wasn't finishing her homework, and she was misplacing her schoolwork. When her teacher asked her to turn in a particular paper, she shrugged and said she hadn't done it. Her group immediately jumped up and said, "Yes you did! We saw you! Don't you remember? We were all working on it!" Two students went to her desk and rummaged around with her until they found it. They had her scribble her name quickly at the top and they handed it in for her. The student was beaming. Even though she really didn't care much about herself or her success right then, her group did care and made sure she knew it. It was just the nudge she needed. It's important to establish a few ground rules for how students will treat one another in their small groups and the larger community of learners. The classroom standards will certainly still serve as the basic guidelines (see Chapter 4). As you move to using group processes more in the classroom, you must determine with your students a social contract for how to interact with each other and do your best to help them internalize it. The following list is a summary of basic guidelines that many successful cooperative learning models use.

Community Ground Rules and Agreements for Group Process

Be Attentive Listeners and Active Communicators

Give whoever is speaking your full attention without interrupting. Avoid other distractions. Use your eyes and body to focus your full attention on the speaker. Regularly share your ideas and contribute your thoughts in a way that others can hear you.

Show Respect to Others: No Put-Downs!

This guideline ensures that each participant will avoid language or nonverbal gestures that put another person down. Demonstrate respect by keeping private things confidential when it is warranted. No gossiping about members of the group outside of the group. When group members are assured that their opinions will be respected and not put down by the others, they will be more likely to share and contribute. Even when this agreement is the only one modeled, maintained, and practiced, it changes the tone and climate of a classroom. (See page 110 for more about classroom put-downs.)

Commit to Respecting Differences and Resolving Problems

Anytime people work together for extended periods, there will eventually be conflict and disagreement. This standard ensures that even through adversity each member stays committed to the process and the group.

Observe the Right to Pass

Occasionally, members will choose not to respond or participate. In other words, they want the right to "pass." Everyone has the right to pass occasionally, with no questions asked. If a member passes regularly or seems resistant to the group or process, then a private problem-solving discussion with you may help resolve the lack of participation.

Share Responsibilities: Everyone Participates

This item ensures that all members agree to find ways to participate actively in the group and the process. It also reminds the strong natural leaders of a group to rein themselves in once in a while and give others a chance to see how they can contribute. Everyone needs to help with the work and responsibilities so no single member is burdened.

Types of Groups

Unit-Long Table Teams or Seating Groups

During a particular unit, you might group students around the particular project or research in which they are interested. These groups are short-term but still require that students adhere to the classroom standards and use the group agreements. If there is no unit of study going on or other way to logically group students, then you might want to create groups that sit together for a month at a time.

Letting the groups decide on a team name is a great way to have them practice brainstorming and decision-making skills. Colors, animals, and environments are always safe bets. You could assign them to come up with team names that reflect the particular unit of study. During a unit on earthworms, for example, groups might name themselves the Super Soil-Shovelers, Garden Good Guys, Compost Wrigglers, Wild and Wacky Worms, or Farmers' Friends. If groups are each studying a different aspect within a unit, then they can name themselves accordingly. During an "Under the Ground" unit at Monarch one year, the groups named themselves Volcanoes, Earthquakes, Caves, Gold, and Diamonds.

Students will become members of multiple groups: seat groups, novel study groups, research teams, and so on. Children should be able to make such statements as, "My family group is the Eagles; we meet on Fridays. My literature learning club is the Mountain Climbers, and we are reading folktales. My math skills group is the Divide and Conquer group. Right now, I sit with the table group that's called Purple People Eaters!"

Learning Clubs

Frank Smith (1986) first described his concept of *learning clubs* in *Insult to Intelligence*. They are comprised of students who have similar needs or interests. Students intuitively understand the criteria for membership; in other words, they know that they qualify as a member of the group. The groups may meet for instruction or to do research together, and the clubs are usually ongoing, although membership may be flexible. A book club is a good example of an out-of-school learning club, and literature or novel study groups are good examples of their in-school corollaries. Students in a class who have similar reading abilities or interests might stay together throughout the year, reading novels or core literature selections. While there is no question that there is an ability-level grouping going on, students also respond to being with students who have similar interests and enjoy peer group discussions and challenges. Learning Clubs might be presented in an invitational way. "Students, may I have your attention please? Anyone who would like a little more help on this map project, I invite you to come join the Latitude & Longitude Learning Club currently meeting at the back table."

Skill or Ability Groups

In these groups, students are assessed and grouped based exclusively on a skill or ability level. Math skills groups and writing process groups are good examples. A key factor is that membership changes at intervals. The students don't feel locked into a group forever. At certain benchmarks in the learning or at certain times of the year, you would do another assessment and participants might change groups. Even if some students feel a stigma about being in a lower skilled group, they also are comforted by the fact that they are members of multiple groups and not just pigeonholed into this one group.

Year-Long Teams or Families

You can also form small groups within your class that will stay together for the whole year. The students will meet regularly to work or do activities, but after the first month, they may not actually sit together in a group during regular class times. In the first few weeks of class, I let students sit where they wish and participate in various activities without assigning groups. After all students have had a chance to work with and get to know others in the class, then they are ready to participate in forming groups.

I use a system I adapted from the Tribes model. Students submit to me individual lists of five to seven names of students with whom they know they would work well. The lists have names of boys and girls. I emphasize that the students on the list may or may not be personal friends; they are students with whom the student knows she can work well. I also let students include on their lists the name of one person with whom they are having conflicts or someone with whom they have had conflicts and don't feel they could work. I assure students that I will try to get at least one person on their lists in the same group with them and really try not to assign the person with whom they currently have a conflict.

Now comes the tricky part. I start forming a profile of the students and their personalities, strengths, and challenges. As I sort cards, I keep in mind that profile and the group assignment guidelines (see list below). I often start by distributing student leaders among the groups. I balance the leaders by distributing the disruptive or less social students among the groups. Then I add other students, keeping in mind my promise to place them with at least one of the students on their lists.

Group-Assignment Guidelines

Each group should have a balance of the following people and characteristics:

- Leaders
- Problem-solvers
- Boys and girls
- Energy levels
- Diversity of backgrounds
- Academic achievements
- Creative and artistic talent

The size of the group can vary. Many programs recommend only three or four students in a group of kindergartners or first graders. In elementary classrooms, groups of four or five work great. Groups of six or seven are more difficult to manage and are recommended only for high school or adult groups.

Make sure that the students know they will be on these teams or with these families throughout the year (or semester). They won't necessarily always sit together or work on every project together, but there will be times throughout the year when they will do things together. With the teams, schedule meetings at least once a week for them to do activities together, to discuss school events, or to make suggestions and plans for upcoming activities. The members of the teams will build almost familial bonds and begin to care about each other.

At Monarch Community School, I was the multiage intermediate teacher. The primary multiage teacher and I created family groups of five or six students that included members from first grade through sixth. The groups met every Friday for an activity, and whenever possible, they did other things together as well. When these two buddy classes went on field trips together, they went with their family group. The students had no questions as to who was in their group. This experience with families or teams has shown me that they work *great*. The students really got to know the others in their groups, learned patience and compromising skills, as well as experienced the power and caring within the group.

Family Teams or Extended Families

When forming yearlong groups or teams, consider including the families of the team members. At back-to-school night or at family gatherings, ask the team families to sit together and get to know each other. You can even build phone trees among the teams. At open houses and family nights, group parents according to these clans to check out what each member of the team has on display. The students who don't usually have family show up feel supported and encouraged by this unique extended family. I've even seen parents offer to pick up kids whose parents were not going to attend and bring them to school functions. "It takes a village . . ."

Short-Term Projects

Occasionally, it may make sense to create a mixed-ability group to work on a project or task. Students may request to be in a specific group. For example, to prepare for a class play, each group would take on one task: create programs, build sets, design costumes, and so on.

Managing Conflicts and Solving Problems

Strategies for Resolution

Social situations can be stressful for many students. Students' roles within a classroom or status among children can influence the brain's chemistry, causing it to release stress hormones in certain situations. Being able to understand what is going on in the brain and body during a conflict may help students manage their emotions and enhance their ability to seek appropriate resolutions. As students experience strategies for solving problems successfully, their self-esteem and confidence increase. Understanding how to manage emotional upsets is a basic coping skill for life.

Reducing Conflicts

If we know that the brain responds to perceived threats in the environment in a way that may impair some students' ability to learn, then we must create systems that can reduce the likelihood of conflicts between or among the students. You can implement systems, such as those described in Chapter 8, to prevent such conflicts. You must also create systems for dealing with conflicts that do occur; such systems will include strategies to resolve and solve problems, ways to manage student upsets, and models for building consensus to ensure that all feel included in the decisions.

People usually have problems due to the following:

Stuff

- Possession of an item; ownership
- Inequality of distribution; having less than others
- Missing items; loss or suspected stealing
- Destroyed property, broken by accident or on purpose
- Lack of materials; not having what is needed

Needs

- Feeling excluded from a group or abandoned
- Loss of friends or colleagues; loneliness

- Lack of power or leadership
- Fear of losing; competition
- Lack of essentials to meet basic needs: food, water, rest, fun, shelter

Identity or Values

- Disrespect shown toward family
- Disregard of or disrespect for ethnicity
- Stereotype of cultural background
- Disrespect of personal goals
- Lack of acceptance for ideas
- Put-downs of physical characteristics or mental competence

In brain-compatible, learner-centered environments, the students not only know some reasonable strategies for preventing conflict but they also have a plan for dealing with any conflicts that may arise. Such knowledge gives students a sense of security that allows them to feel comfortable taking risks and participating fully with other students in the classroom. You and your students will be amazed at the sense of community that develops from these agreements, and students lucky enough to experience this kind of environment will be empowered to create and abide by these kinds of agreements in other situations. Learning the skills for avoiding, preventing, and resolving conflicts will help them throughout their lives.

Urging Messages

This activity is a clear format for sending statements to others in small or large groups. Encourage students to think of something they would like to "urge" another person to do, keep doing, or stop doing. For example, "Robert, I urge you to keep eating lunch with me every day;" "Jason, I urge you to control your humming when you are working, because it makes it hard for me to concentrate;" or, "Lynnette, I urge you to come play handball with us at morning recess." The other student doesn't need to respond. This activity is good to do at morning gatherings, during class meetings, or at end-of-the-day closures. As the facilitator, be sure to limit just how many urging messages any one student can say or receive in a day. Encourage a variety of statements; some will be requests; some, compliments; and others, constructive criticisms. Be sure to model the activity yourself by sending a few urging messages each day.

Preventive Strategies

Standards and Procedures

As I say in Chapter 4, establishing classroom standards and procedures are prerequisites for any learner-centered classroom. Make sure that the standards you select are clear, basic, assertive, and meaningful. On the first day in class, create a motto that reflects standards of behavior. For example, you and your students might come up with "All members of this class will demonstrate respect and responsibility to themselves, others, and the environment." With your students, restate, interpret, and discuss this motto to make sure that *all* students clearly understand its broad meaning. Post it with the rest of your classroom standards so you and your students can refer others to it.

When students know what the expected behaviors are and have a chance to practice them successfully, they are more likely to follow them on a regular basis. Review appropriate procedures prior to each activity until the students have internalized the pattern and programmed it into their brains. When the behavior is stored as a program, the brain doesn't need to use much conscious effort to enact the steps; it's as if it were on automatic pilot. When the majority of the students in the class demonstrate these positive behaviors, conflicts and disruptions will be greatly reduced.

No Put-Downs

Put-downs are disrespectful words or actions that make someone else feel mad, humiliated, embarrassed, frustrated, or sad. Jeff Caplan (1998, personal communication), director of the Santa Cruz based Common Language Program, defines put-downs:

> Put-downs are anything someone says or does that makes someone else feel mad or sad. [They] include

literal statements like "You're so stupid!" sub-literal put-downs like "Oh, yeah, you're my best friend!" said with a sarcastic voice, and nonverbal gestures, facial expressions and mimicry . . . How do I know if it's a put-down? A put-down is defined by the person who receives it. For example, if you say, "Why are you wearing that tee shirt?" to your best friend, it might not feel like a put-down. If you said the same words to someone whom you didn't know so well, it might feel like a put-down to them. (personal communication)

In other words, the person to whom the words or actions are directed is the one who determines whether or not they are a put-down.

An environment that tolerates put-downs will be an insecure place for many. It is at least helpful to consider that the motivation behind a put-down is that it is usually used to help "put-up" the person who is using the insult. People who feel threatened, competitive, uneasy, or just need to prove to themselves how great they are, often sling put-downs around. How, then, do we define and deal with put-downs every day at school?

Turn your classroom into a "put-down–free zone." It takes time, but it's well worth it. To begin, demonstrate just how pervasive verbal and nonverbal put-downs are in our language and culture. Do this simple activity with your students. Videotape a five-minute segment of a popular TV sitcom the humor in which depends on put-downs. After reviewing what put-downs sound like and what nonverbal put-downs look like (eye-rolling, looking away, arms folded, and head cocked to one side), show the video clip. Ask students to tally the number of put-downs they observed in the clip. On a clip I used, my middle school students found more than 40 in less than five minutes! Put-downs permeate our culture so that we become almost desensitized to them, often letting them slide by without commenting.

Give students strategies for dealing with put-downs that don't allow them to engage in the same behavior. Trading verbal put-downs can quickly escalate to a conflict! Figure out systems to make your students more aware of how often they are using put-downs to put themselves up.

What should students do if they hear put-downs? A simple response that Caplan (1998, personal communication) recommends is to say, "That felt like a put-down. Could you say it in a different way?"

You can expand the put-down–free zone to your entire school. Doing so means introducing the rules to the rest of the staff and creating some agreements about not using put-downs yourselves. If the staff cannot live without put-downs during staff meetings, how can you expect children to demonstrate this common courtesy?

Put-Down Paper Doll

Occasionally, if a class is having difficulty giving up put-downs, I have tried this activity. Cut a large figure of a person out of butcher paper, and ask students to use pens and crayons to draw on the features of a generic person. Over a week or so, note every time students put other students or themselves down. Either the person who put another down or a volunteer tears off a small piece from the paper person to illustrate that every time we hear ourselves put down, we lose a bit of ourselves. This visual aid can be powerful, and it really helps students get the idea of the damage put-downs can do over time. Some teachers added another element: as members of the class do things to encourage and support others, they are allowed to replace the torn-away bits.

Essential Agreements: Social Contracts

Essential agreements are usually verbal contracts that people make about how they will talk, act, and behave with each other. They are different from rules in that they don't have consequences tied to them. Such agreements can be very informal, such as when I ask someone to please interrupt me if I've told a story before. That person might otherwise follow common social courtesies and *not* interrupt, perhaps even feigning interest over an already-heard story. Essential agreements and social contracts with friends, relatives, business associates, and students about how we would like them to talk, act, and behave in certain situations help relationships by letting others know what boundaries are important to us.

You might start with social agreements about put-downs. For many years, Susan Kovalik, a popular staff developer, and her associates would say "Ding-a-ling!" if we heard something we perceived as a put-down. In my classroom, we simply said, "Ding!" Of course, we didn't mean the phrase to be *another* put-down; it was supposed to represent a bell going off to alert the speaker that the statement was considered a put-down. The person who said the put-down would usually immediately apologize and set the record straight by restating the sentence in a positive way. Sometimes, younger children have to hear positive options for making certain statements. They can learn to help others restate feelings in positive ways, without using put-downs. I also emphasized that, because we had an essential agreement regarding put-downs, anyone who heard a put-down had the *responsibility* to help classmates restate their feelings in more positive ways. After implementing this procedure regarding no put-downs, you might hear conversations like the following:

Alex: Oh, no, burritos for lunch! They're so stupid!

Katie: Ding, Alex, Ding!

Alex: Well, they are. I hate them.

Katie: Then say that without putting them down, 'cause I like them.

Alex: I wish we weren't having burritos. I really don't like them.

Once students understand that agreement, you might add essential agreements or social contracts that deal with how students refer to the grown-ups on campus. Some schools allow students to call teachers by their first names if the teachers feel comfortable with that. Other schools insist students call teachers Mr. or Ms. So-and-so. Many agreements involve polite language. Are "please" and "thank you" part of the students' everyday language? Or what will you do when students interrupt adults? Under what circumstances is it okay? One teacher I know says that the 3 Bs are the only appropriate reasons to interrupt her: blood, bruises, or barf.

In most cases, the teacher establishes the agreements and social contracts within the classroom. Doing so sets a general tone and gives students boundaries for interactions with each other, something that is especially important in secondary classrooms. As the teacher, establish *your* needs and preferences first then make agreements and contracts with students about how everyone will treat one another.

Following is a list of possibilities for which establishing essential agreements and social contracts may prove helpful:

- The words students will use to refer to one another and to you
- Saying "please," "thank you," and "you're welcome" when asking for or receiving something
- Ways to respond to put-downs
- Borrowing something with or without asking
- Appropriate times and manners in which to interrupt a conversation
- The degree of casual dress that will be accepted (hats?)
- Guidelines for how students will treat furniture
- Guidelines for establishing acceptable seating positions

Class Gatherings

Class gatherings are perfect opportunities for you and your students to express feelings, share ideas, build inclusion, and prevent possible conflicts that seem to be developing. These whole-class conversations are usually informal but regular and frequent gatherings in the morning or at the end of the day. They may be a brief check-in at the beginning of class in a secondary classroom. Sometimes, students share or report on a special activity they're going to get to do. Minor problems might be solved using an "urging message" (see description on pages 109–110). These gatherings are also the perfect opportunity for you and students to share compliments or praise others for recent accomplishments. They are wonderful community activities that build relationships, and you can use them for closure and reflection at the end of the day.

Class Meetings to Prevent Problems

Class meetings are more formal and are usually scheduled just once a week. Establish specific procedures and tools, such as talking sticks and agendas for these meetings (see additional ideas in Problem-Solving Agenda at Class Meetings and "Tools," under Generic Class Meeting Format, later in this chapter). You might train some students to be facilitators, recorders, and timekeepers. In class meetings, your class discusses potential problems and makes decisions ahead of time to avoid possible conflicts.

For example, in one such meeting, students mentioned that several recess balls belonging to the class were missing. They anticipated that pretty soon there would be a conflict over who got to play with the few remaining balls. They made a proposal to send several students to other classes to search for the missing balls and to set up a sign-out system that would guarantee that students all had fair opportunities to play with the remaining equipment. As students see the effectiveness of the preventative strategies, they use them more often and avoid having to use problem-solving strategies later.

Increasing Motivation

Most positive discipline models and brain-based classroom management systems will give many reasons why educators should avoid extrinsic rewards. If it's not the punishment-consequence system ("Do this or here's what will happen to you"), it's the reward system ("Do this and you'll get . . .") that is at the heart of many classroom management systems. Alfie Kohn (2006) says, "Rewards work very well to get one thing, and that thing is temporary compliance" (32). Reward systems can actually insult and damage the caring, democratic community of learners that has been feeling intrinsic satisfaction from doing the right things.

Although some incentives may provide momentary fun, they still can send a wrong message: Do the right thing and you will get a reward. Instead, students should understand that classroom standards and courtesies are expected. They don't have a choice about behaving that way. As DiGiulio (1995) says, "Never materially reward students for cooperating, for respecting others, or for taking good care of their own bodies" (p. 121). That being said, I do know that on a practical day-to-day basis, I have seen tangible incentives with immediate pay-offs used effectively to motivate students. Let's face it: Sometimes we really need temporary compliance! Many children are already so dependent on extrinsic motivation that they may respond to little gimmicks in the classroom in a big way. Some children, especially older ones, actually may need to be weaned off of a reward system if that is how they have been made to comply in the past. I have challenged them for just a day, or a maximum of a week, with little incentives (extra PE time, free choice time, a video, even a pizza party) and made the expectations very clear. I've had these little challenges for cleaning up the room for open house, staying in at recess to finish projects, having all work packets in before noon on Friday, going without *any* conflicts all day. I do not challenge students to upset them or make them anxious, but to put a little pressure on all of us to see if we can "beat the clock." I feel the use of these motivators, especially when I am confident that we have a 90% chance of success, can encourage all of us to kick into gear a little. Incentives, when used sparingly and wisely, can still be motivational techniques. I do recognize the wisdom in what Kohn (2006) says. The more we use bribes and threats to control people, the more we feel we must control them because they grow accustomed to doing what someone else tells them or to rebelling. This really is a form of learned helplessness described in Chapter 3. It takes time and effort to help students find their own reasons to act responsibly and generously.

I use short-term motivational strategies that involve incentives only under the following conditions:

- The students are already dependent on a reward system and extrinsic motivators, and they need some time to make the transition to intrinsic satisfaction.
- I need immediate but temporary compliance from the students, so they can complete a task or behave in a certain way.

- I set up a one-time only wager that playfully challenges students to complete a task or behave in a certain way.
- I am totally stressed out and need temporary compliance to get through the day!

I always follow Jane Nelsen and Lynn Lott's (1994) parameters, though

A friendly, challenging bet may help motivate teens to learn life skills. . . . To be effective, the bet must be made with a friendly, respectful, playful attitude. . . . You can make a bet with your teens without controlling them. (p. 189)

Resolution Strategies

Maintaining Standards and Agreements Consistently

When you make an agreement with your students, everybody involved must be committed to maintaining its integrity and purpose. As the teacher-facilitator of the class, you need to build trust by establishing your dedication to doing so. If you or the students have taken time to create a social contract, everyone should also agree to uphold the ideals within the agreement. Unfortunately, such trust usually means that, in the beginning, you will be the watchdog. If you remain consistent, however, students will begin to demonstrate their commitment to the agreement as well. The brain interprets consistent behavior as security, something that can be counted on, and your consistent behavior will promote the feeling of relaxed alertness in the classroom.

If you and your students agree that no one should put feet on the desk, for example, then you must consistently notice when students are not following this standard. In the beginning, *every time* you see someone casually place feet up on a desk, you must make an observational comment in a calm, assertive, neutral voice: "We agreed that putting your feet up on the desks isn't a (good, healthy, respectful, attractive) thing in our class." You will make the statement regardless of who the student is, even if the student was absent on the day the agreement was made.

The key here is to be a watchdog for only two to three agreements each week. If you have a ton of agreements, it will become tedious to monitor all of them. Recruit other students to give respectful reminders about other agreements. In some cases, the behaviors are just old bad habits, and you and your students will need time to begin to change the behaviors until the more positive behaviors become routine. You can make additional agreements to uphold the other agreements by speaking up and mentioning it to the person who needs reminding.

It's important to avoid embarrassing students, so occasionally I will have private conversations with students who are having a hard time remembering the agreements. We discuss ways they would like me to remind them during class or when in front of other students. We have even worked out secret signals. One class decided that, during times when many of us were suffering from colds, it was annoying and disgusting to have others constantly sniffling and snorting. We also decided that, if you had to blow your nose hard, you should step outside or into a restroom; no one wanted to hear or witness this bit of personal hygiene. Instead of asking someone to "go blow your nose," though, we decided that someone who heard another student sniffling a lot would simply get a tissue and kindly hand it to the sniffler as a respectful reminder.

When one or more students break an agreement more than once, a good strategy for confronting them is to use the following prompts:

- "We agreed that (state the agreement)."
- "I saw (heard, noticed) that you (state the behavior)."
- "Help me understand why you didn't stick to the agreement." Or, "Help me understand what caused you to break the agreement."
- "What can we do to reestablish the agreement?"

I hope such comments encourage discussion about the original agreement and perhaps launch a negotiation about a new and improved version with which all stakeholders feel comfortable.

Identifying the Problem,
Then Letting It Go

We must help students acknowledge that everyone experiences daily conflicts. Conflict is a natural part of life. It is *not* a perfect world. Children often need help identifying a problem and the emotions that come with it. This step toward self-awareness is a key in building emotional maturity. Once we have named the problem and the emotion, then we can begin to decide how we are going to handle it. One very real option to explore is simply letting it go.

For some students (indeed, for many adults, as well), letting something go is a hard task. They are extremely sensitive or have a strong sense of fairness. It is next to impossible for them to let go of an issue. Other students seem to weigh the alternatives in their heads and decide that, in fact, this problem isn't worth getting worked up over, and it is best to let it go. In some situations, these children need to be encouraged to speak up because the problem is too serious to let go. They are sometimes seen as easygoing and unflappable, but may, in fact, be intimidated and fearful about confrontations. Brainstorm examples and discuss with students various scenarios. Students could consider the following questions they might ask themselves to determine whether or not a problem is worth letting go.

- Is anyone being physically hurt right now?
- Does the problem behavior have the potential to hurt someone?
- Is anyone's property getting or likely to get damaged?
- Was the conflict or behavior probably an accident?
- Could you simply point out the standard or agreement that has been broken?
- Can you use your own words, right now, to solve the problem?
- Is the problem one that you have had to deal with before?
- Has the person responsible already apologized?
- Are your feelings just hurt a little bit or are you really upset?

Belvel and Jordan (2003) note how *selective listening* is a powerful intervention technique. They suggest that teachers ignore any behaviors that they determine to be manipulative. "In other words, you refrain from reinforcing the behaviors that you wish would disappear" (p. 179). Use selective listening when students call out, make attention-getting noises or comments, tattle, or make resistant comments such as, "You can't make me!" Teachers will need to be clear about what are simply *inappropriate* behaviors and what are *unacceptable* behaviors. Don't use selective listening for behaviors that can't be tolerated or might escalate.

Problem-Solving Agenda at Class Meetings

A variety of excellent conflict-resolution models are available to schools and classrooms. One aspect of most programs is the utilization of class meetings, which are discussed earlier in this chapter. In many cases, you will facilitate the meetings. In intermediate classes, you may train students to facilitate. While the class meeting may have other agenda items, such as planning events, conducting business, planning fund-raisers, and discussing day-to-day issues, there may also be a regular *problems-to-be-solved* agenda item.

One successful technique for adding problems to the agenda is to post a clipboard or chart. During the week, as students have problems with other students or situations, they can put their own names on the agenda with a key word to alert everyone to the nature of the problem. Ask students not to write the names of the students with whom they have conflicts, just a single word or short reminder phrase about the issue. Figure 5.1 is an example of such a chart.

Figure 5.1

Problem-Solving Agenda, February 13, 2008

1. Joe broken pencils
2. Tara lunch tables
3. Maria computer hogs

When students write down a conflict, ask them to try to solve the problem first by letting it go, talking it out, or negotiating. If the problem is still not solved, then encourage the student to leave the item on the agenda for the next meeting. Occasionally, students will have problems that they don't want discussed in a meeting. In such cases, allow them to write *private* or simply *P* to alert you that they would prefer a private problem-solving opportunity at break or recess.

When the agenda item comes up in the meeting, ask each student whose name is on the list if there is still a problem. If you see one person's name up several times, encourage the student to summarize what some of the conflicts are or to address the one or two that are most important. The issues are often related, anyway. You might also use the strategy of taking up students' first issue and agreeing to come back to their additional agenda items after others have had a chance to share at least one.

In many cases, students have resolved the problem by the time the meeting is called. If such is the case, ask the student to put a line through his or her name. If the problem still needs to be solved, the student states the problem while everyone else listens attentively. If there are other students involved in the conflict, they may state their version of the conflict next. Ask the students involved if they have any suggestions for resolution. If resolution doesn't seem likely, then the facilitator asks others in the meeting to suggest possible solutions. The goal would be to arrive at a reasonable solution to which both parties agree. As the facilitator, restate the problem when necessary, encourage brevity, ask students to state their feelings, and acknowledge these feelings out loud. Be careful to allow others to contribute as needed, without letting it turn into a gang-up session. So often, the problem is resolved just by having it acknowledged in a public forum by being heard. Following is an example format for a class meeting.

Generic Class Meeting Format

Tools

- Agenda: for issues, problems, ideas, suggestions
- Talking stick: item passed around to people who wish to speak; only the person holding it is allowed to speak

---

(Continued)

(Continued)

- Problem-solving strategy: model for mediating problems to which all participants agree
- Decision-making model: method for consensus or voting to which all participants agree
- Clock or stopwatch for keeping time

Ground Rules and Agreements

- Listen actively; use talking stick when speaking.
- Demonstrate respect for all members.
- No put-downs; use compliments and praise.
- Use the right to pass only occasionally.
- Refrain from gossiping about agenda items after the meeting.

Basic Meeting Format and Procedures

- Sit in a circle, if possible; all must feel included and seen.
- Briefly review agreements and procedures.
- Agree about the facilitator's role; is it okay for that person to speak without having the talking stick?
- Choose a timekeeper and set time limits.
- Start with a positive question or inclusion activity for all.
- Allow time for compliments or praise.
- Discuss feelings (see following example).

    Student A: _____, are you ready to hear my feeling?

    Student B: Yes or No

If yes, then:

    Student A: _____, I feel

    _____ when you

    _____

    Student B: _____, I understand you feel

    _____ when I

    _____

Or send an urging message (see pages 109–110).

    Student A: _____, I urge you to

                stop touching my desk every time you go to the sink

                            or

                keep sitting with me at lunch.

- Address agenda items, including problems (prioritize if necessary, and set time limits).
- Close with a facilitator summary.

Mediating Problems and Students as Mediators

When students can't solve problems on their own or in a class meeting, you will probably have to mediate. I have seen some older children acquire the knack for mediation also, but more often, the responsibility will be yours. If you have an agreed-upon method for solving problems, then being the mediator is easy. If there isn't a plan, you will often be put in a position of having to be a judge. The whole dynamic of a problem-solving session becomes two students competing with one another to have an adult judge them to be right in a conflict. It will become less of a win-win session. You will have to become a disciplinarian.

Agreeing upon a method for solving problems is an important step in resolving conflicts. A whole school may adopt a particular conflict-mediation and resolution program, or individual teachers may wish to develop or adopt a method that works best within their classrooms. Figure 5.2 shows one such procedure that I developed that works quite well.

Figure 5.2

Generic Problem-Solving Procedure for Mediator

Step 1: Students involved have taken time to cool off; they are not too upset or crying. They are ready to respond reflectively rather than reflexively.

Step 2: The involved students and you have agreed upon a time and place away from others, with minimal distractions.

(Continued)

Figure 5.2 (Continued)

Step 3: Check in with students to ensure that everyone agrees there is still a problem and that together you all will attempt to find a solution acceptable to all.

Step 4: The first student describes the current problem and states her feelings about it. The second student summarizes and restates the first student's feelings. Remind students to keep statements brief, focused, and current, and help them identify their feelings.

Step 5: The second student describes the current problem from his point of view and states his feelings about the problem. The first student summarizes and restates. Again, prompt, restate, and summarize, as necessary.

Step 6: Briefly summarize and restate feelings of all people involved.

Step 7: Encourage each person to brainstorm possible solutions to this problem. Occasionally, someone will immediately have a short-term idea, then a long-term plan will develop later. Write down all ideas if you think it is necessary.

Step 8: All involved students agree to one or a combination of the possible solutions.

Step 9: Restate the agreement, writing it down if necessary, and get an oral commitment to the solution from all students. Ask them to shake hands, if they feel okay about that.

Step 10: Encourage students to apologize or find another way to make up any wrongdoing or show remorse. Students agree to let the problem go before they return to the class. Remind them that everything said in the meeting is confidential.

The No-Blame Approach

Belvel and Jordan (2003) believe that many conflict resolution models spend too much time trying to figure out what the problem is and who is at fault. They describe a no-blame approach that offers a way to solve students' problems without placing

blame. The standard conflict-resolution model encourages students to state how another's behavior makes them feel. In a way, then, students don't take responsibility for their own feelings; rather, they are placed in the situation of being the victim of another's actions. Their sad or mad feelings are caused by someone else:

"I blame you for my feeling this way." In the no-blame approach, "the problem is the problem" (p. 199). The model acknowledges that the problem certainly affects the child, parent, or teacher, but the focus is on identifying the problem or conflict, not on who did what to whom. As Belvel and Jordan (2003) note, "When no one is to blame and no one is labeled, everyone's task is to simply to solve the problem, and the problem becomes the enemy for everyone—parents, teachers, and students" (p. 199). By focusing on the problem rather than seeking someone to blame, a student may avoid being labeled a troublemaker. When students are identified as the cause of problems, they are stuck with that label, and their good qualities are not always evident. By identifying the problem and not labeling the student, you create possibilities for actually solving the problem.

Handling Student Upsets

Even in the most brain-compatible classrooms, there will be student upsets and unexplained behaviors. When individuals feel threatened, confused, frustrated, excluded, or put down, they will react reflexively; most students' upsets are angry outbursts that are the result of unexpressed emotions. For such times, you need a handful of strategies ready that are not necessarily geared to solving problems. A variety of temporary techniques designed primarily to de-escalate emotional situations exist; select a technique from the following list to which you feel the individual student will respond best. If one doesn't work, try another quickly! Consideration of a child's developmental stage will likely help you select the appropriate response. Remember,  however, that when reacting to emotions, humans are often soothed by actions that would seem appropriate only for young children: a cuddle, soothing words, a bandage!

Touch

Although every teacher must consider each situation carefully, I still recommend the *power* of human contact to soothe and

calm an upset student. As teachers develop interpersonal relationships with students, there should still be appropriate times
in the classroom for a brief pat on the back, a hand on a student's
shoulder, or even what I call a "lean-in side-hug," to demonstrate support and caring.

Listen

Listen with full attention, focused eye contact, and a neutral or
slightly empathetic facial expression. Give simple empathetic
verbal responses such as "Oh" or "I see."

Reflect Feelings

Acknowledge the student's feelings by naming the emotions:
"You are really frustrated right now!" "I can hear that you are
really angry at Felisha!"

Respond

There's nothing better than to have someone jump to your aid
or assistance. With young children, you may need to stop the
interaction or confrontation physically. When students are
really upset, I use my secret weapon—an ice pack! Just about
anything can be de-escalated and comforted with a blue ice
pack. Place it on a physical hurt, or use it to help students who
are simply really upset "cool off"—literally. You can freeze
clean, wet sponges in zippered plastic bags, too. Likewise,
Band-Aids, a drink of water, a blanket, a comfy chair, or for
young children, a lap can all help get the child through an emotional outburst.

While you are assisting students through upsets, resist the
temptation to offer advice, deny their feelings, ask more questions, defend the other person, offer pity, say that you'll fix the
problem, or give a philosophical response, such as "Life is hard,
isn't it?" Such responses only invalidate children's feelings and
may inhibit their potential to solve the problem themselves.
One of the most helpful books about this subject is Faber and
Mazlish's (1999) *How to Talk So Kids Will Listen and Listen So Kids
Will Talk*.

Problem-Solving Role Play

As you begin to create and adopt a problem-solving model, make sure to have some students role-play the steps. Such role-play is a great opportunity for the actors in your class to show their improvisational skills. Ask several students to brainstorm situations that often happen in the classroom or out on the playground. A couple of students role-play possible problem-solving steps. Be sure to display the steps and refer to them as they come up in the role-play. Some students need this opportunity to see what problem solving looks like to feel that they can do it themselves.

Interventions and Short-Term Discipline Plans

Although joyous and exciting places, brain-compatible classrooms may still have inappropriate student disruptions that demand interventions. Unacceptable behavior may require individualized discipline plans.

Take time to discuss with your students the differences between inappropriate and unacceptable behaviors. Inappropriate behaviors are the smaller acts that fall under the heading of *inconsiderate.* Put-downs, putting feet up on desk, and some of the other behaviors I've discussed would fall into this category. *Unacceptable* behaviors are any that physically, emotionally, verbally, or psychologically violate the sense of security and safety in the classroom. Hitting, calling others derogatory names, and many deliberately unkind acts fall under this category. You can usually use interventions to deal with inappropriate behavior. Interventions are really temporary redirection techniques. Use them to "turn inappropriate behavior into appropriate behavior temporarily with the least amount of attention, time, energy or disruption of class time" (Belvel & Jordan, 2003, p. 160). Choose from the list of strategies in Figure 5.3 to redirect inappropriate behavior: If intervention doesn't work, that is, if you see a pattern of inappropriate behavior, you will need to solve the problem by discussing the behavior or giving consequences for it. Consequences for inappropriate behavior should be incremental and individualized, not one-size-fits-all.

Figure 5.3

> **Strategies to Redirect Inappropriate Behavior**
>
> Body language: Use eye contact, neutral facial expression, and proximity to student.
>
> Time and silence: Use "wait time" to alert students to the inappropriate behavior.
>
> Ignoring or selective listening: Selectively ignore behaviors intended to manipulate, engage, or resist.
>
> Broken record: Keep repeating the expected appropriate behaviors.
>
> Move students: Insist on students' sitting somewhere else to change behaviors.
>
> Class meeting agenda: Redirect students to place their names on the problem-solving agenda.

When students do something that is unacceptable, you have only a few choices of what actions to take. Even in cases of unacceptable behavior, do your best to ensure that you are disciplining, not punishing students. Belvel and Jordan (2003) note these differences between punishment and discipline. Punishment is really "control gained by enforcing obedience and order" (p. 167). It is rarely related to the incident and is often threatening and demeaning. "Discipline connotes teaching, learning and instruction. It is training that corrects, molds, or perfects mental or moral character" (p. 164). The delivery of discipline should focus on preventing problems and is neutral, nonjudgmental, and full of positive alternatives.

The list in Figure 5.4 describes a few options you have for dealing with unacceptable behavior.

Figure 5.4

> **Options for Dealing With Unacceptable Behavior**
>
> Consequences: Agreed-upon logical consequences for unacceptable behaviors (not just inappropriate behaviors) such as loss of privileges, detention, cleaning up damage that was done, phone call to parents
>
> Time-out: Agreed-upon time in a designated seat, another classroom, or the administrator's office
>
> Removal: As a last resort, to the office, counselor, or by parent to the home

After trying many techniques in a learner-centered classroom, you may find, as I did, that you occasionally must create short-term discipline plans for individual students who have patterns of either inappropriate or unacceptable behavior. Be sure you have given them numerous opportunities to solve the problem on their own and have also taught them strategies they might use to solve them. Involve parents and the individual students in creating the plan. The plans should usually be short term and directed to very specific, repeated behaviors. Offer some modest, short-term incentives from which the student can select a few. For example, sometimes I note progress on a chart or send a note home to parents. Ensure that students know the consequences for not changing the behavior.

While we can never anticipate every problem or conflict that might arise in our classrooms, we can take a best guess and set up systems ahead of time that give us and our students patterns for solutions. We will experience conflicts with out students, but we can arrive at eventual resolutions by using the systems. We can then begin to count on the success we experience. We actually begin to understand that most problems have a reasonable solution and that there really can be win-win situations.

WHERE TO BEGIN

1. After getting to know students and orchestrating activities that allow them to get to know one another, form long-term family groups or teams. Use the profile mentioned on pages 105–106. Make a commitment to have those teams meet at least once a week.

2. Determine what you consider to be unacceptable behavior in the classroom. Communicate those behaviors to your students. Make sure they know what the immediate action and consequences will be if they engage in unacceptable behaviors.

3. Address put-downs and establish your classroom as a put-down–free zone. Make sure everyone is aware of what put-downs look like and sound like. Make an agreement about how you and your students will address put-downs and the students who are using them.

6

Making a Connection

Building Curiosity and Ensuring Engagement

The brain filters sensory input and is attentive first and foremost to survival issues. In a safe and secure environment, the brain shifts attention to actions that it recognizes as novel and interesting. The brain seeks to make sense of every experience. Attention and emotions are critical to the process. The degree to which we direct our focus, explore relationships, and make connections grows and changes with normal developmental stages. Every teacher and parent has been frustrated by a child's inability to focus and pay attention. However, we must understand that the brain is *always* being attentive to its surroundings. Robert Sylwester (1998) says that, "It's not that they aren't paying attention, they're just not paying attention to you!" By understanding how the attention system is designed, we can better engage it and design our instructional strategies to capture the students' interests.

 **BEGIN WITH THE BRAIN BASICS**

Engaging the Brain

The brain's attention system is very complex. Not only must it evaluate incoming sensory external stimuli, it must also assess memories and emotions generated internally. It can be described as having three layers of complexity (Ratey, 2002).

- *Survival Mode:* The brain first must pay attention to ensure that survival takes place. Making sure one's needs are met will come first. The brain is always sizing up situations to determine the possible risk involved or the possible pleasure that may result. This focus may shift from external input to internal clues and memories of prior experiences. This mode might also trigger the need for movement and the redirection of our senses. We might look towards the input, disengage from what we were doing, and redirect our attention to the new input. We are in a state of *arousal.* We take reflexive action if necessary.
- *Curiosity Mode:* When the brain feels a moderate degree of safety and security, one's attention might be freed up to be attracted to other environmental stimuli: novelty, fun, discrepant events, movement, and things that make us just a little scared and alert. In this mode, the brain is assessing whether or not the novel input might have some reward. (Will this be fun? A little thrilling?) Based on our memories of prior similar experiences, we assign an emotional value to the new input. We direct our attention to the new stimuli.
- *Engagement Mode:* This most developed level of attention requires that the learner use their frontal lobes and executive functions (time-management, organization, decision making, judgment, and prioritization) to override impulsivity and immediate gratification. This complex ability is developed with maturity as well as learning strategies that can help sort, organize, and prioritize new information and experiences. Our brains sustain attention by blocking out irrelevant stimuli. Students are more likely to engage in content when they can see its connections to their real world. Meaningfulness and the anticipation of possible long-range benefits and goals can help the brain pay attention, even when other interesting and fun activities are going on around you.

In general, educators and cognitive neuroscientists agree that a child's ability to maintain sustained focused attention is equivalent to approximately one minute per year of age. (This reaches its maximum at age 18.) Even adult brains are poor at giving nonstop attention without modest breaks and shifts. When requiring students to listen and pay attention, use the following guidelines:

Grades K–2: 5–8 minutes of sustained focused attention (as in direct instruction)

Grades 3–5: 8–12 minutes of sustained focused attention

Grades 6–8: 12–15 minutes of sustained focused attention

Grades 9–12 and adult learners: 15–18 minutes of sustained focused attention

ADD/ADHD

In the last decade, attention deficit disorder (ADD) and ADD with hyperactivity (ADHD) have become the most frequently diagnosed behavior disorders. Students may exhibit a variety of symptoms including impulsivity, poor planning, blurting out without thinking, poor short-term memory, being easily distracted, and having difficulty hanging in there for long-term rewards. With ADHD, frequent movement, fidgeting, and the inability to remain still exacerbate the condition.

To help these students have success in the classroom, teachers will need to design ongoing accommodations as well as teach specific skills to help develop students' frontal lobes. "By maintaining positive emotional states, using challenging and engaging material, and applying strategies that focus attention, teachers can help students with ADHD reach this most productive state of attention and gain the confidence and skills they need to develop goal-oriented behaviors" (Judy Willis, 2007, p.68). The strategies in this chapter can help *all* students build their abilities to function in an engagement mode rather than a survival mode.

Piquing Curiosity

Brain-compatible learning environments are places where students' curiosities are piqued and potential anxiety, frustration, or confusion is diminished. In truly brain-compatible environments, you don't hear children say, "What are we gonna do now?" They already know, or they are part of the process of deciding. They have a sense of curiosity and anticipation, as well as a sense of confidence in knowing a little about what's ahead. In a well-orchestrated classroom, the students are well informed about the agenda, engaged in the process of learning, interested in the next steps, and secure about learning something new. When students are constantly asking, "What are we doing today?" you must ask yourself why they don't know.

Curiosity is defined as "an eager desire to know or learn." If students are curious, then something has probably occurred to trigger their emotions. This arousal of emotions allows their attentional system to zoom in and focus on the source. We know that attracting and holding attention is the key to learning and memory. Margulies and Sylwester (1998) note that, "While intellectual challenge (and even mild stress) can enhance learning, severe short-term and chronic stress shift us into a mode of operation in which we react to danger rather than think rationally about it" (p. 9). In other words, curiosity is difficult to maintain in situations that involve fear or potential threat.

Robert Sylwester also notes that emotions can be aroused by a memory as well as by an event that might occur. Two basic emotions focus on what might occur in the future: anticipation and fear. *Anticipation* is "an expectation; a looking forward to with pleasure." *Fear*, then, would be "a looking forward to with dread." Anxiety is produced when fear blends with anticipation. *Anticipatory anxiety* keeps many students from being able to function in the present. Worrying about what *might* potentially happen, in school or at home, causes students to function in a survival, "on-alert" mode. They are unable to give the learning task their full attention.

Children give incredible nonverbal signals about the range of emotions they are feeling. When they anticipate something, they will often open their eyes wide, lean forward, and possibly hold their breath. When children are curious, they may bring a hand up to the head, look interested, and actually tilt the head. But add something to the situation with which the child is unfamiliar or that has a fearful connection for the child, and you might observe restricted breathing, oral behaviors such as nail biting, tightened muscles, and a closed body posture.

We speak about creating brain-compatible classrooms that are low threat, safe, and secure. Although there are some schools where children are truly in physical danger, more often, children are simply anxious, confused, and frustrated by something that is occurring in the classroom. We must create sufficient interest and curiosity without contributing to students' anxiety and fear. This delicate balance is difficult for any educator to orchestrate.

You can inspire and generate student curiosity and minimize anxiety in at least four ways:

- *Meaningfulness:* Point out connections between the curriculum and students' lives.
- *Organization:* Keep students informed about what is going to happen by posting agendas, calendars, schedules, and plans.
- *Emotional Arousal:* Maintain optimal learning states in which students have opportunities to apply concepts and understanding to new situations; balance acceleration and new challenges with expansion of familiar material and enrichment.
- *Stimulation:* Provide varying stimuli regularly, and balance novelty with constancy.

Create Personal Curriculum Connections

To promote curiosity, make it your goal to provide opportunities for students to make personal connections to what you are teaching. Young students are egocentric enough that connecting any learning to them will inevitably trigger their curiosity. And adolescent and older students, struggling to self-identify, are always questioning relevance to their own lives. Make it meaningful!

We often teach material as though we were just delivering it to students, as if their heads could be opened up and the information just poured into their brains. We feel overwhelmed at the mass of content that we are required to cover; we often charge ahead and neglect to help students see the connections, that are so vital, to their own lives. When we give students a chance to see relevance by recalling a prior experience with similar materials or making an emotional connection to the curriculum, they will be able to leap in and engage! If the material is irrelevant to the student's daily life, or not focused on things that are connected to the student's real world, then the student may never engage.

You can help students connect in two ways:

1. By activating their memories of similar experiences and "hooking" the new learning to this prior experience, and

2. By providing new first-hand experiences.

Introduce new content in a way that connects it to what you hope the students already know. For example, when I begin a unit on reptiles, I discuss reptiles with my students to find out what experiences with reptiles they have had and to bring memories of those experiences to the surface. As students retrieve these memories, the emotions they experienced as they learned or interacted with reptiles emerge as well. Such an activity creates an anticipatory set that you can use to create an atmosphere of curiosity and intrigue about the next lessons, even if they have had a negative experience with reptiles.

Even more effective is actually bringing in items for the students to observe and touch. Students are immediately interested, and their curiosity goes through the roof! Larry Lowery (1989) of UC Berkeley's Lawrence Hall of Science refers to first-hand experiences or dynamic simulations as being the most "powerful learning" that can occur. We must create opportunities to introduce concepts to students through hands-on experiences in class or on field trips. We are notorious for saving the field trip until the end of a unit. But if field trips lend themselves to the most powerful learning, then we should make them the starting point of the entire unit!

During the unit, include centers that have hands-on materials and resource books about the topic so that students may continue to engage and ask questions. As their curiosity is piqued, they should have support materials that allow them to dive into the content and see what else interests them. Place a stack of self-stick notes near a bulletin board for students to write their questions on; others will answer on the notes, as well.

Keep Students Informed With Posted Agendas, Calendars, Schedules, and Plans

You can capture children's attention and curiosity by using simple agendas and calendars that tell them what is going to happen. Not knowing what will happen during the course of the day can create anxiety for many students. Posting a morning agenda can make such students involved, curious, and eager. Posting weekly schedules is also important, especially if there are certain activities students do on certain days of the week. Many teachers find that they are constantly answering such student questions as "Is today the day we go to computer lab?" "Are we going to finish our art projects today?" "Is this an early-release day?" "Are we doing PE outside tomorrow?" By the end of the day, teachers feel as though they have answered the same question 25 times! But just consider the internal process that was going on in the children. They were really unable to attend to the task at hand because they were either anxious or excited about the schedule.

Morning Agendas

You will have a set of arrival procedures in place for when students arrive. They should include coming in, greeting you, putting things away, and so on. The next item should be reading or copying the daily agenda.

Post the agenda where all can see it. I prefer to use two portable (24" × 36"), white, wipe-off boards. I rotate today's agenda board with yesterday's, placed on the floor below. In this way, I ensure that students who are absent a day can go look at that day's agenda. As students become writers, ask them to copy the agenda down into a journal or notebook. By taking time to look at and then write down each item, students are able to pause and visualize what doing that item will entail. Many students will say, "Oh, yeah, I saw the agenda, looks the same as always." But after copying it down, they might say, "Hey, did you see that two more groups get to go to the computer lab today?" I also ask a student volunteer to record an extra copy of the day's agenda and put it in our class's diary (a three-ring notebook with all agendas and classroom newsletters, etc.). It also allows me to refer to earlier pages to see when certain activities, such as a classroom journal, were started or worked on.

Sample Morning Agendas

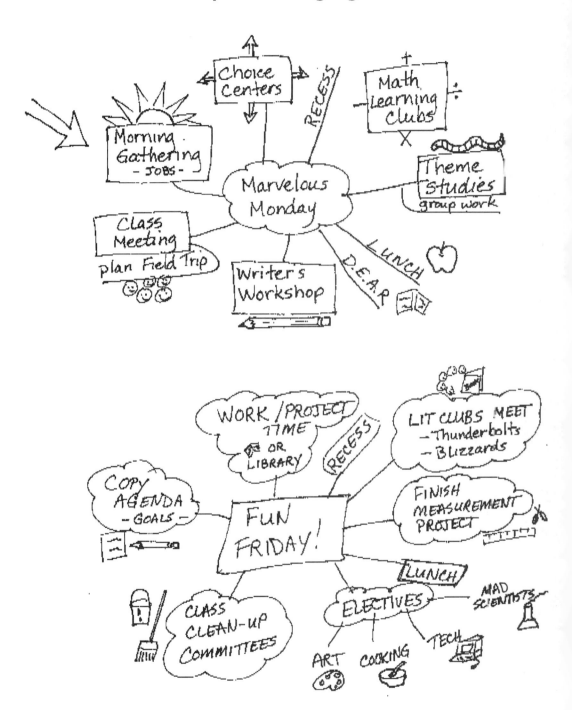

I use a web for most agendas. I write with the same color pen the items that occur every day: morning gathering, recess, lunch, drop everything and read (DEAR), closing comments. Then I write in the items that will be going on during specific days in a different color and add which groups will be doing what. As often as possible, I draw a little graphic to represent the activity. I have developed a few graphic symbols that are consistent with certain activities: a pencil for writing, a book for reading, arrows or a questions mark for choice activities, several happy faces together for a class meeting (see examples on opposite page). I negotiate with nonwriters or slow writers to draw the symbols and write at least one of the words (see examples on opposite page).

You can also use a linear schedule. The main difference between the two is that an agenda gives a general idea of the ways chunks of time are going to be used during the day; schedules get down to the minutia and time table of the day (9:00–9:05 attendance; 9:05–9:15, calendar; 9:15–9:20 review daily schedule). I find that it's easier and saves time to do an agenda and just lump such items together into something such as "morning gathering"; the students know what you do during that time. But a schedule can be particularly helpful if some of the daily activities take place at different times on different days. For instance, I've been at schools that have early lunch on Mondays, Wednesdays, and Fridays and late lunch on Tuesdays and Thursdays. Or, many schools have early release times one day a week. Post schedules with the various daily information so students don't get confused about what to do on which day.

Many primary or special education teachers use photographs as the agenda. I take a picture of students doing each of the types of activities we do on a regular basis: morning circle, centers, PE, computers, and so forth. I print out the photo, put it in a clear sleeve, and attach a magnet to the back. I arrange the photos in the order they will be occurring. Students then have a visual and can note what will be done and it what order. I know some primary teachers who also make little clock faces with the time of each event. You can laminate them and either tape them or pin them next to the activity. Students are able to start telling time by matching the paper clock to the face of the clock in the room to determine when that activity will be taking place.

You can also add a goal-setting activity to the morning agenda. Years ago I incorporated strategies suggested in the Johnsons' (1988) book *The One-Minute Teacher.* After students had recorded the brief agenda in their notebooks, they had to mentally review the tasks for the day then write down one goal for the day right under their agenda. This practice allowed them to focus on what they wanted to have done by the end of the day and to take responsibility for its completion. At the end of the day, students referred to the agenda, marked off the items they had completed, and circled the tasks they didn't get done. Then, they would take a moment to write a sentence that indicated to what degree their written goals had been met.

Weekly Schedules

In many brain-compatible classrooms, teachers orchestrate the curriculum content around thematic units, and they integrate subjects when possible. They might post weekly schedules each Monday and send copies home to alert kids and parents about the flow of the week. Students and their families may generate interest and curiosity by discussing what is coming up. I also try to label some of the lessons and interactions in clever ways that might intrigue students without necessarily giving away the exact nature of the activity. "Creepy Crawly Lab!" for example, will get kids thinking and anticipating much more than "Earthworm Experiment 3" might.

I often provide a weekly contract for older children's notebooks. I write in the specific schedule for their group. By seeing when they will have project time or be able to use the computer, they are able to formulate a plan to manage their time for the week. A word of caution here, however: By providing a superdetailed schedule, laden with all of the assignments due and homework deadlines, you may make a student feel overwhelmed and depressed at the enormity of the expectations for the week. Make sure that agendas and schedules give basic information in a clever or creative format, but they don't become a checklist or massive to-do list.

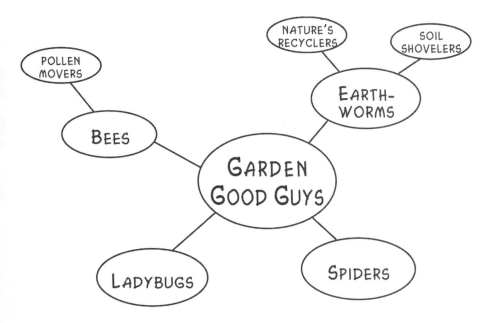

Let Students in on the Game Plan

If you are managing a planned course of study or orchestrating a thematic unit for two to six weeks, take time to create a modified web or chart for the students. Highlight the major topics for each component of the unit. Include basic information about research projects or group activities. Post the field trip schedule and the date and time of the culminating learning celebration. Many children comment on not having any idea when a curriculum unit is going to end. They say that it just keeps going until the teacher's done. Knowing the scope of a unit helps these students maintain focus and interest. Of course, as the teacher, you must be ready to work within a basic framework. Often, a well-designed unit will run over our planned time. Include students in the modification of the schedule, and give them reasons for continuing.

For most of my teaching career, I have used yearlong or semester-long thematic plans. I wrote them up briefly in a web and gave copies to students for the front of their learning log notebooks. Parents got a copy at back-to-school night. I also posted a large version in the classroom. One year, I had a sixth grader join the class mid-year. He merged beautifully into the unit we were currently working on. It wasn't until later that I realized I hadn't reviewed with him our yearlong plan or where we were on that timeline. But he was a smart guy, and after the first week he approached me and said, "I see the year-long theme plan on the board over there. We're working on an 'under the ground' unit that we were supposed to do last month. Are we behind?" Because of the posted clues, he was able to put it all together. He later commented that he was happy we were running a little behind; he didn't want to miss anything because it all looked so interesting!

Balance: Maintaining Optimal Learning States

Emotional states are real biological events in our bodies. Our emotional states can help or hinder our attention and the possibility of learning. Jensen (2006) summarizes four categories of emotional states that are likely to occur in classrooms. "Each of these is a combination of two very similar but distinctive emotional states" (p. 72).

- Fear/threat
- Joy/pleasure
- Sadness/disappointment
- Anticipation/curiosity

Engaging students' emotions is part of what great teachers do. A natural rhythm of a range of emotions is healthy. Curiosity might lead into anticipation that results in joy! It's important for teachers to see ways that they can influence students' emotional states to optimize learning.

- Use movement and physical activity to stimulate a learners' state. Even brief bursts of opportunities to play a game or role-play can change the physical state of students and create some positive emotions, especially for the bodily-kinesthetic learner.
- Orchestrate a discussion or debate that has at least two sides. Generating a little friendly controversy and providing opportunities to express opinions always generate some emotions.
- As described in Chapter 3, take some time to laugh and have a little fun.
- Use storytelling and the sharing of personal anecdotes to encourage empathy and feelings.

- Change the pace of instruction in the classroom. Create a "deadline" or some mild pressure to increase interest.
- Create an opportunity to have some "inconsequential competition." Play some games that emphasize the curriculum. Highest point getters could have some minimal rewards.
- Demonstrate enthusiasm and excitement over the activity.
- A ritual or celebration at the beginning or ending of a class can influence students' emotions. Include a musical selection, a cheer, a call-and-respond motivating motto, or a quieter moment-of-silence circle.
- Ask students for a suggestion of a preferred activity from a previously generated list as an energizer. Allowing the class to decide how they might change their own learning states is very empowering.

Use Novelty and Varying Stimuli

If you want to get students' attention and get them involved in a given activity, create a variety of instructional strategies to "hook" them. To get someone's attention most quickly, you need to do or provide something that contrasts to what you are already doing or what students can easily predict. You might try teaching from the back instead of the front of the classroom. Or try a new seating arrangement to liven things up a bit. Play new music as students enter the room. Or turn the lights off and close the curtains to change the mood.

In certain classrooms, the teacher or a student each day hides a certain item related to the theme somewhere in the room. When students arrive the next day, even the most recalcitrant of them are immediately hooked into searching the room for the item. The activity was clearly only an attention-getting device. But if you can get their attention for a few minutes, you've won half the battle.

(KWL) Know; Want to Know; Learn

This tried-and-true strategy has been around in many forms for a long time; its simplicity is the reason it works. As an introduction to a topic, ask students to brainstorm what they already *know* about it. This discussion encourages students to search for their personal connections to the topic. Then generate questions as to what the students want to know. At the end of the unit, review the questions, and ask students to record what they *learned*—a simple, yet tried-and-true strategy for triggering curiosity.

Mystery Box

This strategy works especially well in primary classrooms, but don't underestimate its power in upper levels, as well. Wrap an old box with a removable lid with wrapping paper. Place an object or a piece of paper with the name of an object or animal written on it in the mystery box. Students play twenty questions. Generating only yes-or-no questions, they try to guess what is in the box. They must guess within twenty questions. Help children see what kinds of questions will be most helpful.

Countdown

If there is a special day coming up, put the number of days left until the event up on the board. We had a day to celebrate division, and the countdown said, for example, "D-Day: 13 days left." This kind of daily check-in serves as a reminder and builds interest and anticipation.

WHERE TO BEGIN

1. Post a daily agenda for all to see. Make it an extremely simple web with symbols or a linear schedule. Give your students and yourself a chance to review the agenda at the beginning of the day/class to build enthusiasm and diminish anticipatory anxiety. Review at the end of the day to celebrate accomplishments and prioritize next steps.

2. Go through your lesson plans and choose at least five for which you can easily note personal, relevant connections for your students. Don't leave it up to chance for your students to make the connections! Create a door into the lesson by having an informal discussion with the class that gets them talking about what this concept has to do with them. Create hooks!

7

Meaningful Experiences

Creating 21st-Century Citizens

Brain research over the last 35 years confirms that we construct our own understandings about the world around us through experiences, activities, and processes that have emotional and social elements. To build a deep understanding of any subject—from baseball to biology, from plant life cycles to politics—students must have opportunities to explore. It is through manipulation, experience, and process that the brain internalizes, makes connections, and remembers concepts. We are learning more every day from cognitive neuroscience research regarding the importance of guiding children to develop social and emotional skills through firsthand experiences.

Schools in the United States are currently experiencing an imbalance within the curricula. Accountability, and to a large degree funding, are determined by students' test scores. The mandates of NCLB have prompted districts to become stringent curriculum monitors and to utilize tools such as pacing guides to assure that teachers *cover the content*. Because of the emphasis of literacy and basic skills on the high-stakes tests, many schools have reduced time in other valuable school subjects and activities. So now at the beginning of the 21st century, a student's school experience may not include very many opportunities for visual and performing arts, physical education, projects, field trips, or community service. Teachers simply don't have the *time* to devote to these (often) nontested subjects and activities.

I meet with teachers all over the country expressing their concern over the reduction and loss of these valuable school experiences. While the acquisition of facts and knowledge is important, there is too much emphasis on memorization rather than *understanding*. When students become *active* learners, they will be better prepared to transfer what they have learned to new problems and settings (Committee on Developments, 2000).

In my workshops, I often ask teachers to recall a powerful learning experience (PLE) that they have had in their lives. I define a PLE as a time when you learned a whole lot in a short amount of time and you can still recall it now. Many remember learning things like driving a car, learning a new sport, mastering a new hobby, and so on. Some of the PLEs are from school experiences. They are usually things like musical or drama performances, art class, home economic projects, sports activities, mock trials, dances, field trips, and so forth. I've never had anyone say, "Wow! That phonics worksheet in third grade was really powerful!" We remember events more completely that involved us *doing* something and making an *emotional* connection.

This kind of deep learning is referred to by Caine, Caine, McClintic, & Klimek (2005) as "immersion of the learner in complex experience" (p. 107). Orchestrating meaningful multisensory experiences in an enriched environment is one of the key elements of a brain-compatible and learner-centered classroom (see Chapter 1). These types of project-based, experiential, learning opportunities are difficult to fit into such regimented curriculum designs that many teachers are experiencing today.

Authentic Tasks

I urge teachers to keep searching for golden opportunities to link school skills and curriculum content to real-world projects and activities. Try to find ways for students to do real things that are meaningful to them and are worth doing. These can be called *authentic* tasks. Authentic tasks are significant and have purpose. The activities and student products are *genuine.* An easy way to determine if a task is authentic is to consider whether or not a student would want a significant person in their life to come to school and see the resulting product or performance. When students make projects that are "keepers," it means that the task was important and meaningful to them.

The need for more meaningful, authentic curriculum projects is a huge issue. The types of activities and tasks would be different at various grade levels. The selection of authentic tasks would be unique for each community and school. To be meaningful and relevant, it might be a beach clean-up project for Monarch School or a tiger mussel abatement campaign in Holland, Michigan. Creative teachers and curriculum teams need only to look outside the school's door to begin to see possible authentic learning opportunities.

For the purpose of this chapter, I am proposing that there is a complex experience that every teacher at every grade level can, and should, take time to orchestrate. *Democracy* is one concept students must experience to be able to comprehend its meaning and be able to apply it to daily life. Every classroom has opportunities to create authentic experiences with the democratic process. Learning how to make change happen, participating in shared decision making, and working within a committee are all ways that students can experience and learn about the democratic process. We should be integrating these skills into every curriculum, within every classroom, at every grade level.

The Process Is the Point

Students' learning will not be powerful, nor will they be able to access it easily, if they experience the concepts and skills only in secondhand ways. Anytime someone or something other than the students themselves interpret new information, via lectures, demonstrations, pictures, videos, readings, the learning loses depth and complexity. The least powerful learning takes place when the concepts are third-hand, that is, abstract or symbolic via notations, numerals, letters, words, or icons.

Inviting students to be part of making some of the decisions in the classroom may at first seem frightening to many educators. If we give children power, then who knows what they will or won't do? If we are truly attempting to create learner-centered classrooms, however, we must consider developing systems that include students as active participants. There is no question that the bulk of the curriculum may already be determined. There are also many schoolwide structures and systems that may be mandated and perhaps are nonnegotiable. But it is our job to orchestrate as many opportunities with which we feel comfortable for students to become problem solvers and decision makers.

In 1916, John Dewey published his classic *Democracy and Education*. In it, he writes that if we are to maintain our democratic society, we "must have a type of education which gives individuals a personal interest in social relationships and control, and the habits of mind which secure social change without introducing disorder" (p. 115). If our nation is going to continue to maintain a democratic way of life, our students must have real-life experiences with democratic processes and the responsibilities that come with participatory governing systems. When young students have had authentic opportunities to effect change, make a difference, and contribute in school settings, it will be more likely for them to participate as an active voting citizen when they get older.

Simply learning about democratic ideals through a textbook or even via a one-time mock election will not guarantee the deeper understandings that students will need to apply democratic principles as participating citizens in the real world. Michael Apple and James Beane (1995) describe two ways that schools can bring democracy to life: "One is to create democratic structures and processes by which life in the school is carried out. The other is to create a curriculum that will give young people democratic experiences" (p. 9).

> We live in a democratic society, and students need practice at functioning in such a society. Often, too many teachers give students practice at surviving in an authoritarian atmosphere (perhaps because the teachers fear anarchy). (Nelsen, Lott, & Glenn, 2000, p. 53)

In what activities and classroom decisions are you willing to have students participate? How can you create meaningful opportunities and allow students to generate their own ideas about developing events, planning activities, and setting policies?

What Kinds of Decisions?

Your individual situation will dictate to what degree the students in your class will be able to make decisions and shape policy. In many schools, the administration seems to mandate *all* policy, even that within individual classrooms, at least at first. Many teachers say that there are very few areas in which students might generate ideas and make decisions. Often, after a little investigating, you might find that you have more flexibility than you first thought. Your administration may be willing to consider well-thought-out ideas that students present in a professional, mature way. Besides determining which decisions your administration will or will not allow, you also need to reflect on the areas in which you are willing to give up some control and allow students to make decisions.

Places to Start

Consider some type of class event or activity. Later, the class might begin to plan larger events that encourage participation by the whole school. I like to focus on celebrations, fund-raisers, and community service events. Before you begin, you also have to decide which elements of the planning and decisions you will leave up to the students. You may want them to organize as much of an event as possible, including taking on all of the following responsibilities:

- Getting administrative approval for the event
- Scheduling the event on the school's or classroom's master calendar
- Advertising and promoting the event
- Planning the details of implementation, such as getting a microphone and prizes, planning an assembly, setup, and so on

Determine in what areas you will allow students to participate and plan. The following descriptions are good places to start.

Celebrations

During class meetings, encourage students to put on the agenda opportunities to plan parties, celebrations, and family gatherings. Often, a group of students will suggest the class have a party on the day before a long school break. They form a planning committee and decide who will bring what for refreshments. With your approval, they can plan games, costume contests, watch videos, and so on. I have always encouraged students to plan such parties well ahead of time and, if possible, to relate them to something we've been studying.

I often put family gatherings on the agenda for students to help plan. We usually organize these celebrations of learning as a culminating event for special units of study or when students have completed projects (see Chapter 9 for more ideas). I try to have at least three or four such gatherings a year. Students have set up museums, art shows, performances, information booths, and interactive stations. We invite all family members and friends, as well as other members of the community who have some connection to what we have been studying. These gatherings are always wonderful community-building events.

Schoolwide Events

Encourage students to brainstorm, plan, and organize some kind of activity suitable for whole-school
participation. Theme days, such as Backward Day,
Crazy Hair Day, or Spirit Day, are great ideas. You
might also plan food drives, red ribbon weeks, and
Earth Day celebrations. Initiating and planning these
activities is especially helpful for the school if
there isn't an active student council to organize
them.

Community Service

Keep your eyes and ears open for ways to help out within your
community. One winter, a local group requested donations for
motel-size soaps and shampoos. They were donating them to
homeless shelters and church groups that were making up toi-
letry bags for the needy. We saw the article in the local paper,
and a group of students made up a flyer for the rest of the
school. In a short time, we had collected a couple of boxes of
supplies.

Looking for similar opportunities may fall on your own
shoulders at first. You may want to take the initiative and
then give over the planning to your students. As students and
their families get the idea, soon other suggestions will come
in as to ways the class can help. Early in the school year, for
example, there is always a beach clean-up day in our area. To
be assigned to a local beach, I had to call and put our name on
the list during the summer. Once school started, I announced
to the class what part of the beach was ours. I said they could
decline to participate or plan the rest of the activity on their
own. They chose to plan it! Fifteen years later, I read in the
local paper that Monarch School was still participating in the
beach clean up. Those students had started a community service tradition! This time, the classes had created a huge sculpture made from the trash and it was displayed at the local
museum.

MONARCH OPENS CLEAN-UP EXHIBIT

(*Santa Cruz Sentinel, Sept. 28, 2008*)

Last year, students from the Monarch Community School, an alternative public school, cleaned beaches to raise awareness about the impact of plastic waste on seabirds, which are at great risk of choking because they mistake plastic in the ocean for food.

An exhibit of work created by Monarch's fourth- and fifth-graders opened recently at the Santa Cruz Museum of Natural History, 1305 E. Cliff Dr., in conjunction with California Coastal Clean Up Day. The exhibit includes a nearly 6-foot-tall tree made of plastic that students collected from the beach, as well as a display of bolus, or regurgitation from albatross, which included a measurable amount of plastic. (Monarch, 2008)

Fund-Raising and Social Causes

Often, students will decide to do some kind of activity to raise money for the class, for a local charity, or for a major social cause. Students in my class wanted to raise money for the class account, which went for field trips and other expenses or for whatever cause in which we were currently involved. They recognized the opportunity to have a bake sale every Wednesday at their lunch recess for the high school students at the adjoining campus. Different students helped each week. Often, a parent helped supervise. Believe me, there's nothing like a hungry high school student to wipe out inventory!

During a unit on marine mammals, my students decided to raise money at the family gathering. Each research group had a booth and sold small items (magnets, bookmarks, buttons, food, etc.) for less than a dollar. They wanted to send the money they raised to the charity that supported the animal they were studying: Save the Whales, Manatees, and Dolphins.

Handling Bigger Responsibilities

In a brain-based, learner-centered environment, our goal as educators is to facilitate opportunities for students to take on more responsibility in daily classroom decisions. The reality is that many students, especially older ones, are not able to handle the challenge immediately. In some cases, they have come to your class having had little success in previous classrooms. They may lack self-management and basic social skills and be suffering from learned helplessness. If others have always managed their behavior through rewards and punishments, they are often not capable of accepting the new, greater responsibilities we are asking them to take. As agents of change, we must carefully assist students to make the transition to responsible human beings.

When we teach children how to make good choices and give them opportunities to do so, we give their feelings of capability and self-esteem a boost. At school, just as at home, the shift from having adults making all the decisions to the children's beginning to make decisions for themselves should be gradual. It takes time. In addition, young children should be given opportunities to make only those choices that are appropriate to their developmental maturity.

There are many things to consider when encouraging children to take a role in planning tasks. There are two main rules parents and teachers must follow as they guide children toward making decisions and taking on responsibility:

1. Children should not be allowed to make decisions in which irresponsible choices have potentially dangerous consequences to themselves or to others.

2. Never allow children to make decisions that you can't live with. For instance, don't give students the impression that all decisions they make necessarily will be implemented and become part of policy if that simply isn't a distinct possibility.

Many teachers in schools and classrooms that have made the transition to more democratic procedures love to tell war stories of what the first year was like. When students are suddenly asked to be cooperative participants before they have mastered the basic social and emotional skills necessary, chaos can result. On the other hand, many students will immediately rise to the occasion. As Kohn (2006) notes,

> Just as it takes the eyes a moment to adjust to the sunny outdoors after emerging from a dark room, so it takes the mind and heart a while to cope with freedom after having been expected to do what one is told. (p. 96)

Over time and with some success in making decisions about topics that don't have huge repercussions, students will acquire skills, and their confidence will increase.

Bigger Decisions

As students practice solving problems and making greater decisions, you can increase their responsibilities. At various times, I have placed students in charge of a variety of program choices, process decisions, and even curriculum selections:

- Organizing the schedule for the day or week and figuring out how to work on the "must-do" activities while allowing time for "may-do" activities
- Setting deadlines for assignments and minimum requirements for projects and products
- Selecting and arranging themselves in work groups for special projects
- Creating selection criteria for their participation in certain activities
- Developing a rubric for assessment of their work
- Researching and investigating community resources for in-class presentations
- Designing systems for rotating use of special supplies or computers
- Determining content for parent communications or press releases
- Determining consequences for those who keep others from learning
- Suggesting areas of emphasis in the content for the next unit of study

With content standards so delineated, be cautious about appearing that you are turning over too much of the curriculum for student input and direction. Because we have so many standards to address and so much pressure to teach "the basics," I still prefer to orchestrate as much of the curriculum as possible around unit themes. Then, within the topic areas that I select, I encourage the students to develop areas of interest and related special projects. In this way, I refrain from directing all of the content and curriculum, but certainly I have ensured that I am addressing the curriculum requirements for that grade level.

Decision-Making Possibilities

When students are discussing in small groups or when the class is meeting altogether, decisions will come up that must be made. Many times, a simple majority vote taken by asking students to raise their hands seems like an absolutely perfect method for making decisions. It is efficient. In a heartbeat, you can determine whether or not a proposal has the support of the people. The problem with voting yea or nay is that there are inevitably winners and losers. If the decision is not one in which anyone has a lot at stake, then the losers will usually accept the decision peacefully and participate in the decided course. However, if the vote is close or if the stakes are high, be ready to deal with disgruntled losers.

Many new decision-making methods are being explored throughout workplaces, in schools, and even in governments. These methods are usually designed to gain consensus and promote various ways that participants can feel they have influenced the final decision in some way. Negotiations and compromise, when possible, become key factors in the process.

Gradient System

I have often used this method for making decisions in my classrooms. Use a one-to-five gradient (or one-to-three for younger students) to allow participants to express their level of support for a given proposal (see the samples on pages 156 and 157). When you present a proposal, everyone in the meeting states a number that corresponds to the level of support they are willing to give to it. At Monarch Community School, the adult decision-making committees (leadership teams, curriculum committees, and parent groups) used an almost identical gradient to the one students eventually adopted.

Use a gradient when someone makes a proposal (see Figure 7.1). If several ideas are being proposed, then the decision makers must consider each carefully to determine which one has the most support. First, ask a student to read the proposal aloud, and then the facilitator restates it or writes it on the board. The process is similar to that for making a motion during a meeting. The facilitator asks if anyone needs any clarification in the language or other aspects of the proposal. Then the facilitator asks, "Are you ready to make a decision?" Students respond by using a thumbs-up sign, nodding their heads, or even quickly answering "yes." If someone isn't ready, then continue the discussion until everyone understands the proposal (see also Back-Up Systems on page 160). Participants then show how much they are willing to support the project by stating a number from the gradient, either orally or by holding up the appropriate number of fingers. In a shared decision-making model, there is less of a need to have secret votes. The idea is for everyone to know how everyone feels about a given topic and for there to be no surprises. Following is the scale used at Monarch School and the corresponding degrees of support.

Figure 7.1

Team Decision Gradient

5. I love the idea! I think it is the best solution. I will support it completely.

4. I like the idea. I'm supportive. I have positive feelings about most aspects.

3. I can live with the decision. I'm ambivalent about the results. I have no strong feelings for or against.

2. I do not really care for the idea. I'm not in agreement, but I won't stand in the way.

1. I strongly oppose at this time. I will make attempts to stand in the way.

Determining Support

A strongly supported decision would be one for which most members cast a four or a five vote. Everyone loves the idea or

at least really likes it. Even if a small percentage of participants give it a three, it still has the potential of being strongly
supported.

If a large percentage of the participants say that they can just
"live with it," don't consider it a strongly supported decision.
While technically it may have passed, it does not have the support of the people. Living with it does not mean that people will
defend, support, work, volunteer, or aid in implementation.
Such decisions are immediately evident in that many people
vote two, a few vote three, and a very few vote one. At Monarch,
we agreed that, if someone gave a one to a proposal, we would
not go forward until that person could be convinced to raise the
level of support or until the proposal was revised. When someone gave a proposal a one or a two, then the facilitator would
ask, "What would it take for you to give it a three?" Such a
question gave the participant some responsibility to come up
with a compromise and a solution, not just block the decision.
Many times, the compromise is in wording or a small detail that
others overlooked. Once you revise, you start the entire voting
(decision-making) process over. While this process may seem
tedious at first, it gets easier as people practice it.

A three-point gradient may work better for younger
students (see Figure 7.2).

Figure 7.2

Three-Point Gradient for Younger Students

3. I really like this idea! I want to do it!

2. I don't really care one way or the other. It doesn't matter to me right now.

1. I really don't like this idea. I don't want to do it.

I have seen some large classes or groups use strategies to
determine a mathematical average using the numbers. They
determine a number below which the proposal does not pass.
For instance, in a group of 10 people, if 4 said they were a five,
2 said four, 3 said three, and 1 person said two, the average

would be 3.9. In that group, perhaps they said that the proposal needed to be at least a 3.5 to pass. It is a good idea to determine up front how much support you need for a given proposal. If the proposal is about major changes in policy or program, then it most likely demands a strong buy in by all stakeholders; you certainly wouldn't want the consensus to be "We can live with it."

A True Story

At Monarch Community School several years ago, the students organized and put on a marine mammal fair as a culminating activity on a unit of study. Each multiage group (kindergarten through fifth grade) had five to seven members. They were organized based on interest, and each group had to have a variety of ages and abilities. They all had to research their animal (gray whale, manatee, walrus, dolphin, sea otter, orca, sea lion, or elephant seal) and put together an information booth for the evening fair. Each booth had to have brochures, fact sheets, a display board, artwork, and something to sell to raise money for the species. Students made small magnets, earrings, bookmarks, and badges. The most popular item was food. The gray whale group made soft pretzels in the shapes of plankton and shrimp, the gray whale's favorite food. The manatee group sold cups of "manna tea" (hibiscus herbal tea). The walrus group made clam chowder (clams are a staple of the walrus's diet). Each group sold items for no more than 50 cents.

The evening was a huge success. Many families and friends came to see the incredible displays the students had created. Some groups made more money than others, ranging from $22 to more than $60. As the groups looked at their individual efforts, they realized that the money combined would total more than $350. Some young voice in class spoke up and said that we should combine the money and give it to some local group. This brilliant student quoted me, saying, "Remember what Ms. K. says, we're supposed to think globally, act locally!" I could have hugged him! Many other students agreed that it was a good idea, but many felt that they had already made an oral commitment to the original charity and weren't sure it would be right to change. We needed to have a class meeting, discuss this possible change, and make a decision.

For the next intermediate class meeting, we put a proposal on the agenda: "All groups will contribute their booths' money to one classroom sum to donate to a local group." Students from the primary class who wished to participate were invited to join the meeting, too. The students brainstormed a couple of issues. Would it be fair to the people who had made purchases, thinking their money was going to one cause, to send it to another? To which local group would we contribute this big amount? Most students quickly noted that, as long as the money went to a cause associated with marine mammals, we didn't have to worry about misleading our patrons. Deciding which group to give the money to was more difficult. We live on Monterey Bay, and the number of ocean conservation groups in the area could wash you away. Someone finally suggested that we donate the money to our local (six blocks away!) UCSC Long Marine Laboratory. We had all visited the museum and the interactive "touch tanks" on numerous occasions, and we knew they were doing lots of research on sea lions, elephant seals, whale migration, and sea otters.

Even though everyone participating in the discussion seemed to think this proposal was a good one, we still needed to make a formal decision using our five-point gradient model. We wrote the proposal on the board: "We agree to pool the money made at the marine mammal fair and give the whole amount to our local Long Marine Lab." We went around the group, asking for opinions from more than 30 students.

The response went something like 5, 4, 5, 5, 4, 4, 5, 5 . . . until we got to Chris. Chris said, "One." Our facilitator responded appropriately: "Please tell us, Chris, what it would take for you to vote three on this proposal?" Third-grader Chris replied that he had been reading the newspapers lately and knew that there were some controversial new buildings going up on the property near the lab. He didn't want our money to go to help fund the new buildings. When we asked him how we could change the proposal to ensure the money didn't go for the new buildings, he asked, "When you make the donation, can you ask

them to use this money only for the museum and not for building any new buildings?" Others also felt this stipulation was a
good one, and we added the statement to the original proposal.

Now as we went around the circle, the support was higher
than ever, and when we got to Chris, he said, "Five!" Of course,
he would: He had changed the whole idea! He had protected
the endangered land and saved the class from having made a
horrible charitable blunder!

As we neared the last of the group, we came to Steven, who
said, "One." "What would it take to make it a three?" He
replied, "I don't know; I don't have any more money to
donate." When we explained that he didn't need to donate any
money, we were using the money from the fair, he quickly
changed his opinion to a five. Yeah! We achieved a consensus.
Students held fists up into the air and shouted, "Yes!" and a
cheer erupted.

The two students who challenged the proposal are examples
of participants you might find in adult groups. Chris didn't
share pertinent information during the discussion. He often
liked to create drama by waiting until the last minute to put a
monkey wrench into the process, thus delaying the consensus.
It seemed as though he timed his sharing of information to
make himself look like a hero for knowing it, rather than sharing it during the discussion so the group could take it into consideration. I've seen many teachers on staff committees do the
same thing. Steven, on the other hand, is the group member
who is present but whose mind wanders. He is somewhat apa-
thetic, maybe because he doesn't really feel included. By asking
him to explain his vote, we forced him to get clarification, thus
empowering him as a part of the decision-making body.
Questions such as the one we asked Steven work with adults
who are not paying close attention as well.

Back-Up Systems for Consensus

It is important to have strategies to fall back on should the consensus model get hung up in some way. If you have attempted
to reach a consensus, and for some reason the decision continues to be weak (threes), or one or two individuals are blocking

it, then have a default system for determining what to do. Many groups decide that if they spend a certain amount of time discussing and voting and cannot reach a consensus, then they will go with whatever proposal gets a simple two-thirds majority vote.

If time constraints demand you make an immediate decision, then you should also have an understanding about who will be responsible for making a decision for the group. If a class is getting used to making many of the decisions, they may not like it if you suddenly step in and take over. However, if you have discussed the possibility ahead of time and everyone has agreed that, "Teacher makes the decision if it needs to be made before our next class meeting," then everyone will be able to live with it.

The Committee System for Classroom Management

Student committees can take over many little (and big) jobs as easily as can an overworked teacher. For many years, I used committee systems in my classroom to facilitate students' involvement with organizational duties. I found this program to be popular in my classes, and students had heard about it before they even came into my class.

The success of this system is based largely on the students' daily experiences with group-cooperation activities. The more they work together on related projects, the more the idea of taking over some housekeeping duties will seem natural, and students will eagerly complete such tasks.

Divide students into four heterogeneous groups on the first day of school, and assign each group to one of four tasks (see lists below). During each of the three remaining quarters, redivide the students into four new groups (or keep the original groups if they are successfully working together) and rotate the duties.

I had the committees meet once a week for 30 minutes, usually on Friday mornings just before our regular class meetings. They kept records of decisions they made and of individual students' assigned responsibilities. They shared this information during committee reports. They often met again during recess, at lunch, or occasionally after school to complete all of their tasks. They met with me when necessary. Following is a list of possible tasks to assign to student groups.

Maintenance Engineers

- Empty trash and recycling daily
- Clean sinks and counters
- Feed classroom pets
- Straighten the take-five corner
- Take the lunch count and attendance to the office
- Water plants

Communications Specialists

- Answer intercom respectfully
- Answer the door
- Go to the office and carry messages
- Pass out papers and other supplies
- Write and publish at least one issue of a class newsletter during the quarter
- Write thank you notes to guests who have come to the class

Special-Events Coordinators

- Plan for guest speakers to come to class
- Assist with field trip preparations
- Plan a science-experiment day
- Plan a theme day (for example, tourist, twin, backward)
- Plan a cooking day or a shared potluck meal
- Make arrangements for any special events being planned by the class, including fund-raisers

Entertainment Planners

- Arrange for videos to be shown in class that pertain to the curriculum
- Nominate a DVD/TV/VCR monitor to set up equipment
- Tell class about upcoming TV shows that pertain to the curriculum or theme

- Give periodic movie reviews
- Provide technology updates regarding new devices or programs that would be appropriate for kids
- Make up and perform a skit, puppet show, or variety show for the class

Kids' Social Action

I highly recommend books by Barbara A. Lewis. Her *The Kid's Guide to Social Action* (2000) has tons of ideas and suggestions about guiding children to become involved in community projects. The last third of the book is filled with resources: addresses, forms, survey templates, and guidelines for press releases. These are wonderful springboards into taking action in your communities.

Team Effectiveness

Take time to assess how well the democratic process is working with your students. At midyear and again at the end, ask the students to respond in writing or discuss some of the following reflection topics:

1. Responsibilities were shared among the group's members.

2. Decision making was shared and promoted consensus.

3. The meetings were organized and we kept to an agenda.

4. As a group member, I voiced my opinions on issues.

5. As a group member, I accepted the different ideas of my teammates and attempted to work with them.

6. I willingly volunteered to accept responsibility for a class project.

7. As a team member, I accepted decisions and helped support them. (Also see "Team Member Survey," page 206.)

Consider using a rubric (an example is provided at the end of this chapter). After students have had experiences with one you have provided, let them design a new rubric.

WHERE TO BEGIN

1. At a class meeting or gathering, encourage the class to share in organizing a theme day. Use a simple majority vote to determine the theme. Help students brainstorm all the elements they need to plan the day successfully: location, participation, promotion, times, prizes, judging, rules, and so on. Help them form a committee or assign tasks. Start small! Make sure they choose something playful, but reasonable. You want them to experience success the first time. After the event, orchestrate a discussion to evaluate the day and determine whether it was a success. Use the information to plan an even more successful theme day.

2. Take time to teach a gradient decision-making process to your class. With the students, create a simple proposal about changing an everyday occurrence, such as the way they line up to come into class or the way they decide who gets to use the computers. Lead students through the gradient decision-making process, and then ask them to abide by the decision for a trial period of one week. Encourage a discussion after the trial period to determine if they want to make any changes. While the first proposals shouldn't be too important, it is wise not to have meaningless exercises just to use the process.

Rubric for Teams and Groups

For each statement, select the ranking you believe best reflects that group member's efforts and contributions.

5—Always demonstrates the quality

4—Frequently demonstrates the quality

3—Sometimes demonstrates the quality

2—Seldom demonstrates the quality

1—Never demonstrates the quality

1.	Takes active role on initiating ideas or actions.	1	2	3	4	5
2.	Is willing to take on responsibilities.	1	2	3	4	5
3.	Sensitive to the needs and feelings of other members of the team.	1	2	3	4	5
4.	Helps promote team spirit and has a positive attitude.	1	2	3	4	5
5.	Is willing to frequently share ideas and resources.	1	2	3	4	5
6.	Respects differences of opinions and backgrounds, and is willing to negotiate and make compromises.	1	2	3	4	5
7.	Provides leadership and support whenever necessary.	1	2	3	4	5
8.	Acknowledges other members' good work and provides positive feedback.	1	2	3	4	5
9.	Produces high quality work.	1	2	3	4	5
10.	Helps meet team's deadlines.	1	2	3	4	5

8

Student Choice in a Learner-Centered Classroom

Orchestrating Opportunities

When students have choice and are allowed to control major aspects of their learning (such as what topics to pursue, how and when to study, and outcomes to achieve) they are more likely to self-regulate their thinking and learning processes than when they have little or no choice or control.

—McCombs & Miller,
Learner-Centered Classroom Practices and Assessments

When we give students choices and opportunities to control the content and process of their learning, their motivation increases. When they are highly motivated with low stress, optimal learning can occur.

BEGIN WITH THE BRAIN BASICS

Empowerment: Freedom to Choose

When we perceive a choice, our brain chemistry changes (Ornstein, 1991). Research indicates that when learners look forward to doing an activity and feel as if they have some control over the type of task, they feel positive and motivated. These feelings trigger the release of endorphins and dopamine, neurotransmitters that promote a general sense of well-being and confidence. Having choices allows the learner to feel more in control. Feeling in control of one's learning experience contributes to self-determination, self-confidence, and empowerment.

The prefrontal cortex (PFC) lets you weigh out different possibilities and consider options. If you have a mature, healthy brain, your PFC allows you to suppress some emotions and make more objective logical decisions. Two other areas of the brain that appear to help us analyze data, ask questions, be skeptical, and determine facts from opinions are the basal ganglia and the cerebellum. The occipital lobe may assist you in visualizing the outcome; and the motor cortex (near the parietal lobe), with the mirror neuron system, will help you get a feel of what the choice might be like when selected.

The left and right hemispheres of the brain process incoming information slightly differently. The left will tend to process information logically and rationally. The right hemisphere will interpret the data within the context it's presented. Often, people tend to depend on one side over the other. This could influence how they make choices.

Analyzing data, creating a visual representation, comparing the selections to prior knowledge (matching to our existing schemas), adding an emotional response, and then predicting possible outcomes are all aspects of how the brain integrates information and stimuli to make a decision. Researchers report that having too many choices may overstimulate the brain and create anxiety.

Research: *Learning and the Brain: A Comprehensive Guide for Educators, Parents, and Teachers* edited by Sheryl Feinstein, Rowman & Littlefield, 2007.

Practical Application: *Learning Smarter: The New Science of Teaching* by Eric Jensen, Corwin Press, 2000.

Web Site: Wired: http://www.wired.com/science/discoveries/news/2002/04/51839

The Choice Challenge

One of the more challenging offerings classroom teachers can give students on a regular basis is the opportunity to choose. In a *brain-compatible, learner-centered* classroom, students having choices is a nonnegotiable. As we attempt to educate our students in traditional school settings and under the NCLB mandate, the task of giving students choices in what they can learn, how they will learn it, how they will demonstrate their understanding, and how to express themselves seems overwhelming. The job would not seem quite as difficult if we were sure that the students already knew how to make appropriate choices. But we fear that if we give students freedom to make their own decisions regarding learning, they will abuse the privilege and make poor choices or actually choose not to learn!

To alleviate our fears, we can begin to learn how the brain makes choices. There are many strategies for structuring and limiting selections, so students can make good choices. We must understand the following:

- How the brain detects a pattern, selects a program, and makes choices
- How to guide children in making appropriate choices
- How to structure curriculum choices to allow for a wide range of student abilities, learning styles, and intelligences
- How to limit choices to help children select processes
- How to provide choices that build children's self-esteem

How the Brain Makes Choices

Leslie Hart (1998) describes the brain's process for making decisions, going into action, and ultimately learning. Learners must first evaluate the situation, task, or need (observe, detect, and identify the pattern or patterns); otherwise they simply do not know what the problem or task is. When given choices and situations in which they have no prior experience, relevance, context, or personal meaning, learners do not observe a connection and therefore don't even recognize any viable choices.

In other words, they aren't likely to implement programs for which there is no frame of reference. Many times, I have heard teachers lament the fact that students never choose a particular station or center. After some reflection, we often determined that the students didn't really understand what the activity was or its purpose; while it may have made sense to the teacher, it didn't have a meaningful context for the learner.

Another problem arises if we always direct students; we have no way of knowing if they are able to detect patterns, select programs, and implement them. As students have opportunities to evaluate, select, and implement their own choices that reflect their own personal connection, they will become more confident with making choices. If they are suffering from learned helplessness (see Chapter 3), or if students have been overdirected, they may mistrust their own abilities for evaluating situations and making selections. Hart (1998) defines the first step of learning this ability to make choices as "the extraction, from confusion, of meaningful patterns"; the second step is "the acquisition of useful programs" with which to implement the learning (p. 132).

Humans repeat what Hart calls the pattern-program cycle of learning thousands of times a day. The brain receives input through all the senses, matching the external clues and cues to its stored memories and patterns and making its best guess as to the most effective program to implement. When a stored program doesn't work in the new situation, creativity comes into play, and through trial and error, we construct new programs to store.

Simply stated, students must *detect, select, try,* and *modify* when making and implementing choices. Following is a description of each of these steps.

Detect—Identify a pattern, a problem, an option.

Select—Analyze possibilities, determine a strategy, and make a commitment.

Try—Go into action, implement a strategy, make an attempt.

Modify—Creatively adapt strategies to fit new situations; adjust and combine known patterns of action to construct a new program.

Discovery Play

Not all choices and experiences in the classroom must have immediately discernible patterns or be based on every student's prior experiences. Indeed, especially in primary classrooms, many choices and centers will simply have objects that invite discovery play. Interesting games, manipulatives, toys, and real-world objects will get children's attention and may or may not have a specific learning objective or product attached. The entire point of having *choices* is for students to have an opportunity to experience the objects and start to recognize patterns associated with that experience.

Students can engage in discovery play alone or with others, without any prompts or with a facilitator's encouragement and inquiries. It is through these free-exploration periods that students learn to construct their own knowledge based on previous experiences. Brooks and Brooks (1999) note that constructivism occurs when children are allowed the freedom to explore, inquire, construct relationships, and search for their own understandings rather than follow other people's logic.

Mary Baratta-Lorton (1976) and her husband began the Math Their Way program over 35 years ago. They have always insisted that children need to have ample time to freely explore learning materials that they may use later to help them understand skills and concepts: "Without free exploration children's play interests are unsatisfied, and until this need is fulfilled, the children will pursue this priority relentlessly" (p. 2).

During free explorations and discovery play will be a wonderful opportunity for the teacher to observe and document what kinds of tasks the student chooses to do with the materials. In the Math Their Way program, instructors might look for

- Which *materials* were selected,
- What *patterning* did the student spontaneously begin,

- What level of *intensity of interest* was demonstrated, and
- What *verbalizing* did the student do about the exploration?

But of course, there must be some guidelines for presenting reasonable choices so that students don't feel overwhelmed. Faced with many frequent decisions, brains may show signs of fatigue and disinterest (Amir, 2008). This is easily observed after students have taken long tests filled with multiple-choice responses. They are exhausted. Going out for a meal after a long day of work can be tedious if the menu is filled with so many choices that I can't even make logical decisions!

Limiting Choices

It seems logical that if providing students with choices increases engagement and motivation then more choices would be even better. But in the case of offering students opportunities to choose, more is not always better. Opinion varies greatly regarding how much personal choice students should have when it comes to learning. With our focus on standards and state-mandated curricula, we rarely have any flexibility in allowing students to determine *what* they learn. However, we should still offer students many opportunities to choose *how* they learn skills and concepts (process) and a variety of ways to *demonstrate* their understanding for assessment (products). Over the years, I have seen two extremes, neither of which is effective:

- Classrooms offer no choices; all students do every activity directed by the teacher. The classic one size fits all.
- So-called free or alternative classrooms in which there are an overwhelming number of learning centers or activity areas around the room; children are encouraged to "Go, be free, and learn"; there are few requirements.

Recent research has shown that from the brain's perspective, it doesn't matter which you choose—*just being able to make a choice is reward in itself.* The neurons located in the pleasure center of one's brain have been observed producing endorphins when just provided an opportunity to make a choice (Hopkin, 2007).

Must-Dos and May-Dos

To assure accountability, it is helpful to develop a balanced program of "must-dos" and "may-dos." You will have activities, processes, tasks, and experiences that *all* your students must participate in and complete. Perhaps you want all students to experience the same process so that students have a common understanding when you give them extension activities. You will also sometimes want all students to complete a similar task and have a specific finished product as a summative assessment.

I often gave *all* students in my class a specific assignment: a book-writing project, self-portrait, multimedia project, math game, novel contract, or research report that they had to complete by a certain deadline. I expected all students to meet the same basic guidelines for each project. I didn't give them much choice about the activity itself, but they could often choose the specific content within the project or report. These must-dos often served as benchmarks, summative evaluations, or portfolio pieces for assessment. Because the standards being addressed were the same for all, we developed a common rubric to evaluate them.

Within the required assignment, teachers may want to *tier* the task based on students' readiness, interests, and learning profile. This key instructional strategy of a differentiated classroom acknowledges that some students may not be ready to complete all aspects of the task with the same degree of complexity. So even within a must-do assignment, there might be accommodations, modifications, and extensions designed for several types of learners.

In addition to the required task for all, teachers may often have some additional tasks that involve student choice. May-dos could be a choice of several different types of extension or enrichment activities related to the unit or a lesson. While the tasks should be somewhat equal in scope, and in time and effort needed, they may be more open ended to encourage students to elaborate and create unique responses.

Beginning Choice

Not only are children's school experiences directed, their home life and afterschool time are often scheduled and planned as well. This problem crosses socioeconomic boundaries. Children in affluent families are often shuttled from activity to activity, with weekends filled with performances, sports, and community activities. Children in impoverished communities are often housebound after school or in organized daycare programs. Neighborhoods are sometimes so unsafe that children are allowed only to stay inside and watch TV. There aren't as many opportunities for children to explore and make their own decisions about free time. Since many children have no practice at making choices, introduce them to the process gradually.

In the beginning, give students only a few choices. Young children may not be developmentally ready for more than a few options. Even older students who have been in tightly organized and directed classrooms may be overwhelmed with too many choices at first. To start, include activities that offer the same degree of difficulty. Remember, though, to include activities that address a variety of learning styles and intelligences. Structure them in such a way as to allow for a wide range of abilities. Some teachers begin introducing choice through homework assignments.

Three examples of choices in assignments appear on pages 175–177. The first is a Homework Assignment for a thematic unit on flight and the Wright brothers in an intermediate class (see Figure 8.1). Notice that there are only three tasks from which to choose. There is also one opportunity to work with a partner. Students can earn the same number of points for all assignments. The expectations about what should be included are clearly stated. There is no obvious benefit to choosing one over another.

Figure 8.1

Homework Assignment on the Wright Brothers
From Monarch Community School

Choose one of the following. Each is worth up to 10 points. You may work with a partner only on item 3.

1. *Draw* a picture of the Wright brothers' airplane, the *Wright Flier.* Use 12-by-18–inch white paper; color the picture. Include all major details of the design.

2. *Dramatize* in a one- to two-minute skit for the class what Orville might have said or thought during the historic 12-second flight and immediately afterward.

3. *Compose* a poem or lyrics to a song that commemorates the historic flight. Include references to the plane, the people, the location, and the flight itself. Be prepared to present it to the class.

The second is the culminating assignment for Scott O'Dell's *Island of the Blue Dolphins* (see Figure 8.2). The examples clearly include opportunities for students to express themselves artistically, dramatically, musically, and verbally. Students may comment on the fact that one appears easier than others, but you can use this statement to lead into a discussion about the multiple intelligences and how not all students are working at the same level.

Figure 8.2

Culminating Assignment for Scott O'Dell's *Island of the Blue Dolphins*

After reading the novel, follow the instructions below. Be sure to do your *personal best.* Use *lined* paper for *writing* and *unlined* paper for *drawing. Put your name and the date at the top of each page.* Record the inquiry number of each item you respond to. Put all your hard work together in a *decorated folder.* Complete at least six of the following items.

1. In a well-written paragraph, *compare* the villagers (Karana's people) to the Aleuts. Note at least five ways that they are alike and different.

(Continued)

Figure 8.2 (Continued)

> 2. Skim Chapter 6. In a short paragraph or in a detailed drawing, *describe or illustrate* what the villagers had done to prepare for the Aleuts' return.
>
> 3. *Describe* the events that took place when Karana had to go back for Ramo. Or *draw* at least three scenes that show what happened.
>
> 4. *Imagine* that you are Karana. *List* the fears you would have if you were left on the island. *Tell* some ways that you could overcome your fears.
>
> 5. In Chapter 10, Karana makes a decision to turn back the canoe. *Tell* what decision you would have made and why.
>
> 6. *Draw* a detailed picture of Karana's new house as it is described in Chapter 12.
>
> 7. *List* as many items as you can that Karana had to make while alone on the island. *Evaluate* the items to decide if each was a necessity or a luxury. Next to each, *note* which you think it is.
>
> 8. *Describe* and *list* all the animals Karana had as friends or "family." *Rate* them according to which you like best. Organize the list, putting the ones you like best at the beginning.
>
> 9. Karana demonstrated many traits: creativity, caring, perseverance, common sense, and responsibility. *Choose* one of these traits and *tell* about instances from the story in which Karana shows this trait.
>
> 10. *Draw* a headstone for Rontu's grave. *Write* an appropriate epitaph for it.
>
> 11. *Describe* some of the natural disasters that occur in Chapter 27. Or *draw* a picture of what Karana might have seen.
>
> 12. *Describe* in a short paragraph what you think Karana's thoughts and feelings are as she leaves the island.

The third example shows a variety of ways that students might make a presentation about a book they have read. A popular strategy of differentiated instruction is to present the choices in the form of a Tic-Tac-Toe board (see opposite page). Students are to select three tasks that are in an alignment vertically, horizontally, or diagonally. The board's choices could change regularly to include a wide variety of popular products. For this type of generic activity list, the required criteria should be posted for each type of task so that students know what the product will involve and how it will be assessed. I also like to note what kind of "smarts" (Multiple Intelligences) are emphasized as well as what level of thinking is begin used (Bloom's). For an expanded list of possibilities see page 190.

Tic-Tac-Toe Board for Literature Study

Choose and complete three in a row: Horizontal, vertical, or diagonal.

Comprehension	*Evaluation*	*Synthesis*
Summarize key events in the story using a mind map with colorful graphics or icons. **Logic & Picture Smart**	*Recommend* (or not!) this book as a novel to be on the list for next year. Submit it as a letter. **Intrapersonal & Word Smart**	With a partner, *create* and *demonstrate* a game show based on elements of the story. **Interpersonal, Logic, Body Smart**
Synthesis	*Analysis*	*Knowledge*
With a partner, *create* an epilogue for the story that takes place 20 years from the ending. **Interpersonal & Word Smart**	*Analyze* the ending of the story using a PMI (plus-minus-interesting) graphic organizer. **Logic Smart**	*List* descriptive words or phrases from the book for each of the characters. (Give page numbers.) **Word Smart**
Knowledge	*Comprehension*	*Application*
Make a minidictionary of 10 unusual words or phrases from the novel. **Word Smart**	*Describe* character traits of at least three characters from the story. Use your own words. **Word Smart**	*Draw* a colorful picture of a dramatic event in the story. **Picture Smart**

Several experiences with these kinds of choices will give the students a sense of trust, security, and consistency—all brain-compatible elements! Another benefit is, after seeing some of the products that the other students come up with, they will be more willing to try activities that challenge them. Soon, you might expand the list, varying the ability levels and perhaps giving more points or a higher grade to some. Some of the choices might be open ended, with less structure and more room for creativity and student inspiration. Such opportunities require students to analyze and evaluate more to make decisions and choices; they must choose based on their strengths, their abilities, and the grade they are attempting to get, as well as on other criteria.

Remember that a student will rarely choose something with which her brain does not have experience unless she has acquired enough confidence in her abilities over time to risk choosing a variety of tasks. For example, if you include creating a triorama of a scene from a book as a choice, but you have not discussed what trioramas are or constructed them in other contexts, you run the risk that students won't have any experience or a context for trioramas; their brains won't interpret and recognize it as a true choice. At first, make sure that the selections on a list or in centers are similar to those you have done in class before. Once students have a pattern of making successful choices, they might be comfortable taking a risk on a choice with which they are not familiar, choosing to find out what it is and making it.

Triorama

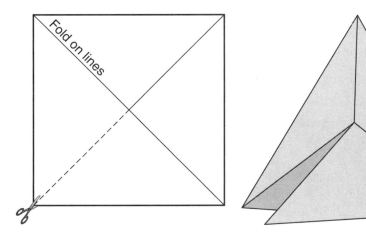

Homework Choices

An excellent way to incorporate choices into students' daily learning is to have self-directed homework assignments, such as the one below. Susie Phanton, a multiage primary teacher in Santa Cruz, California, created these homework choices. Prepare a list of possibilities each week from which students can select activities to do at home (see example in Figure 8.3). Make sure parents understand that their children are supposed to choose from the list. Explain this policy at a back-to-school night or in a brief note home.

Figure 8.3

Weekly Homework Choices: Friendship and Cooperation

From Susie Phanton

We are beginning our study of friendship and cooperation. Please choose at least one activity from each group of choices. Put a star by the activities you do, and turn in this paper with your completed choices on Friday, October 16, or Monday, October 19.

Writing Activities

- *Interview* a friend. Write five questions and record your friend's answers.
- *Write* a story about you and your friend.
- *Write* a letter to a friend. Address the envelope.
- *Write* a poem about a friend.

Reading Activities

- *Read* a story about friendship, such as *Frog and Toad Are Friends.*
- *Find* and read some poems about friendship.

Math Activities

- *Play* a game with a friend that involves math, such as Yahtzee, Monopoly, or Pig.
- *Make* a graph of the degree to which you and your friends like something.
- *Write* several word problems about you and your friends.

Some students may need suggestions for what to do each day, not just "By the end of the week, complete four activities." If students have only had directed homework assignments before, they may need help creating a weekly schedule. For an example, see "Weekly Spelling Tasks" on page (180).

Weekly Spelling Tasks

Due Date: _____

1. Students will copy their spelling words for the week on Monday.

2. Students will complete the following tasks as homework:

   - Write each word four times.

   - Study words by spelling them out loud.

   - Take a practice test at home.

3. Complete at least *two* of the following activities:

   - Alphabetize the words.

   - Select five words and use each in a sentence.

   - Find at least six words or the letters in magazines or newspapers; cut them out, and glue them to paper.

   - Create a crossword puzzle that uses at least six of the words.

   - Use toothpicks or string and glue to construct at least five of the words on paper.

   - Use all the words in at least three sentences, and use those sentences to write a paragraph that makes sense.

   - Write five words and draw a picture that represents each word next to it.

   - Look up five words in the dictionary, and write a strong definition for each.

4. Complete all tasks and turn in the work with the Friday work packet.

Primary Choice Centers

In primary classrooms that are already designed around centers, teachers are usually able to create systems for some choices. Even in classrooms where three groups of students are simply doing three different activities, you can work in a way to allow for some may-dos.

Choice Boards

Schedule students for three or four center rotations, and allow them to choose their last one. Display the assignments for centers on a board with labeled clothespins, tongue depressors, or 3-by-5–inch cards in pockets. As students arrive in the morning, they check the center board, determine where they will begin that day, and select something they may do. They take their name stick or card and place it at the sign for the center they would like as their free choice. Limit the number of students in each choice center; the first four, for example, get to be in that center. If you have students who are chronically late, they may be motivated to get to class early or on time because that may be the only way to get into the centers they want. If tardiness is *not* their fault, be sure to let them occasionally choose on the day before.

Passports or Center Schedules

To facilitate the rotations for a whole week, some teachers print out and post a schedule for the various student groups each Monday. Students can see their group assignments (see Figure 8.4) and know where they will be during the rotations (see Figure 8.5). Students keep them in their learning logs, in a pocket folder, or in their supply bins as they travel to the different activities. In the example below (see Figure 8.4), the class has been divided (tiered) into three equal groups of eight students: Earth Group is working at grade-level expectations, Sea Group needs some modifications and adaptations, Sky Group is generally working at a more complex level. Within each of these larger tiers, there are two subgroups. Within these smaller groups, four students can be clustered for specific learning needs such as English language support, reading and vocabulary support, or students with advanced capabilities. In the schedule below (see Figure 8.5), there are four centers in action and one guided reading group happening during each 30-minute section (A-B-C). After the Monday and Wednesday rotations have been completed, all students will have participated in each center at least once.

Rotation Schedule from Monarch Community School

Figure 8.4

Sea Group # 1	Earth Group # 1	Sky Group # 1
Student 1	Student 1	Student 1
Student 2	Student 2	Student 2
Student 3	Student 3	Student 3
Student 4	Student 4	Student 4
Sea Group # 2	Earth Group # 2	Sky Group # 2
Student 5	Student 5	Student 5
Student 6	Student 6	Student 6
Student 7	Student 7	Student 7
Student 8	Student 8	Student 8

Figure 8.5

	Monday	Computer Station	Spelling and Vocabulary	Choice Centers	Writing Workshop	Guided Reading Ms. K
A	10:05–10:35	Sea 2	Earth 2	Sea 1	Earth 1	Sky 1 and 2
B	10:40–11:10	Earth 2	Sky 2	Earth 1	Sky 1	Sea 1 and 2
C	11:15–11:45	Sky 2	Sea 2	Sky 1	Sea 1	Earth 1 and 2

	Wednesday	Computer Station	Spelling and Vocabulary	Choice Centers	Writing Workshop	Guided Reading Ms. K
A	10:05–10:35	Earth 1	Sky 1	Earth 2	Sky 2	Sea 1 and 2
B	10:40–11:10	Sea 1	Earth 1	Sea 2	Earth 2	Sky 1 and 2
C	11:15–11:45	Sky 1	Sea 1	Sky 2	Sea 2	Earth 1 and 2

Free Choice Time

Many teachers have discovered that it can be difficult, especially in primary classes, to have some children doing must-dos and others doing may-dos at the same time. What seems to work better is to have students do their required rotation first, then have specific times for free choice. Some students actually go back to centers where they needed to complete some work. Others, like my youngest son, loved this time of the day because they got to do what they wanted without worrying about completing anything! Of course, you need to have a system in place that ensures fair time at all the centers. Often, the fastest, most aggressive students get to the blocks first, or some students take over the computer stations every day. We had a rule that a certain group of students had first choice on certain days.

Some centers might always be available in your classroom: computers, art, drawing, listening. You can also create seasonal or special-project centers. I rotate certain materials every couple of weeks. I put Legos away for a month or so; when I brought them back out, they were a hit all over again. You can put away puzzles, games, manipulatives, dress-up trunks, even certain books for a while, then reintroduce them. By rotating items, you keep children from doing the same things every day and encourage them to try new things.

The HighScope
Program Alternative

The HighScope Educational Research Foundation is an independent nonprofit organization, established in 1970, with headquarters in Ypsilanti, Michigan (see www.highscope.org). The HighScope Program for early childhood education takes a more radical approach to choice in the primary grades: They have actually built an educational approach based on the belief that children learn best when they can choose. Emphasizing "active participatory learning," students construct their own knowledge through direct, hands-on experiences with people, objects, events, and ideas (HighScope, 2009). Students meet in small groups with an adult facilitator to discuss what they want to work on. They make a commitment, then have a work time at the appropriate center that can last up to an hour. The centers might have art materials or manipulatives that students can explore freely, or several may have activities based on a class unit. When the work time is up, students return to their groups; individually, they tell what they learned during their work time.

Managing this program can be quite a complex task. Teachers continue to move around the centers to prompt, ask questions, encourage, and help children process what they are doing. In some cases, teachers are actually noting students' participation and progress on a record sheet. The teachers are constantly looking for the teachable moment. At other times during the day, they might do a lesson based on what insights a few children discovered in a center.

Guiding Students' Choices

As I mentioned earlier, one reason teachers are often wary of giving students opportunities to choose what they learn and how they learn it is that we know there are those who don't seem to rise to the challenge and ultimately make poor choices. We know that, although they appear to be trying, many students have a difficult time consistently making good choices. Following is a list of some common complaints teachers have.

- Students always choose the same center or activity; perhaps they even dominate the center.
- Students seem always to choose activities that don't challenge them.
- Students don't really choose anything; they wander around and often disrupt others.
- Students seem to choose only "fun" activities, such as art, drama, or play, and they avoid anything that involves writing, reading, or projects.

Before I talk about how to take action and when it's necessary to do so, I want to caution you about assuming the student is being lazy or choosing activities that don't challenge.

Students need times in their day during which they can experience self-determination and build self-confidence. Their choices will be based on their own needs, desires, and preferences. Some will need to do the same activity over and over to build self-esteem and feel empowered doing something at which they are successful. By letting children do the same thing over and over, you allow them to become an expert at that task. We all have such tasks we enjoy and work on because we're good at them: hobbies, crossword puzzles, golf, quilting, running, and so on. We never become bored doing these things.

You should, however, take action in a couple of situations. If a child is dominating a center and other students are not getting to participate fully, then guide that student to allow the others to participate. If that doesn't work, guide him to make other choices. I always try to determine if the other students truly need the student to move on rather than rely solely on my own observations. Many students love having the expert at their center; it puts them in good company: "We like it when Matt is here; he always comes up with great ideas for the blocks!" or, "When Kurt is with us at the computer station, we know we have someone to help us if we need it." It also builds students' self-esteem to allow them to help other students, which is always a good characteristic for your students to develop.

If I decide I need to do something, I tell the student that she has had a lot of time at the center. I honor how successful she has been and how good she is at the task; then I insist she choose from one of the other centers for the next few days. You can negotiate or bargain with the student, but make sure she understands that the other students need her to move on for a while.

When students are choosing activities from a list, such as the inquiry lists on pages 186 and 188, they often repeatedly select only those they think are easiest. Use the list as an opportunity to discuss the probability that the task requires them to use one of their most developed intelligences. I was the kind of student who always chose tasks that involved performing and presenting. Being a strong interpersonal and bodily-kinesthetic learner, these types of tasks always seemed easiest to me. I would keep choosing them until someone encouraged, asked, prompted, requested, or demanded that I try something else. From those personal experiences, I know that students develop a variety of skills if you occasionally require them to choose a task that demands they use one of their lesser developed intelligences.

If I have a student who needs a nudge to try something new, I often just cross out a few of the choices on the list and discuss with the student why I'm doing so. Avoid making the request sound punitive. I always let students know how successful they have been with the choices they have been making. I also reassure them that I want them to be the best, well-rounded learners they can be. Students and I will often set goals for how long or how many times the choices will be limited before they can go back to truly free choice again.

Yearlong Theme: Keepers of Our Earth

Monthly Unit: "In the Pond"

Inquiry Projects: May-Do Choice List

Due: _____

In addition to *writing the essay,* "What I Learned," and *answering the key questions,* (Must-Dos), select the appropriate number of required *inquiry projects* from the list below. Choose carefully, and do your *personal best.*
  Sea and Sky groups choose one project; Earth group, choose at least two.

1. *Create* a colorful poster that illustrates the life cycle of a frog.

2. *Create* a mobile that illustrates a food chain that might be found in a pond.

3. *Carve* or *sculpt* a pond animal out of wood or clay; share it with the class. Be prepared to tell something about the animal.

4. *Make something* useful out of tules that would help in the daily life of the Ohlones.

5. *Write, define,* and *illustrate* at least 10 pond and herpetology words for a children's dictionary. Use good paper and colored pencils or crayons. Spiral bind the book, or make copies, if you choose.

6. *Interview* a naturalist, water biologist, herpetologist, or park ranger. *List* at least 10 questions and their answers.

7. *Compose* and *perform* a song about ponds or things you learned during our unit. You can make up words to a familiar tune if you prefer. Be prepared to present to the class.

8. *Memorize* and *perform* for the class a pond play or puppet show. Ms. K has two from which to choose, or you can write your own. You may work with one or two other people on this one.

9. *Draw* at least four scenes from our literature selection, Kenneth Grahame's *The Wind in the Willows*. Include scenes that are about river or canals. Bind your illustrations into little books if you wish.

10. *Research* blue-green algae as a food source for humans. Present your findings to the class. Bring in a recipe using algae or some to sample.

Some students seem to avoid choices that involve certain tasks or skills, such as writing or reading. Students may also avoid activities that require them to interact with other students or expect them to draw or use their bodies. I have often used systems that require students to choose from various categories of activities. It looks kind of like ordering from a Chinese restaurant: one from column A, one from column B. I group writing choices on one list, art choices on another, and performances on yet another. I then require students to choose one item from each list. See, for example, *The Wind in the Willows* assignment in Figure 8.6.

Figure 8.6

The Wind in the Willows Book Project Due _____

After reading *The Wind in the Willows*, select and complete the appropriate number of projects from the following lists. Do your *personal best*. Assemble written inquiries (from List A) in a decorated cover. Spelling, sentence structure, and comprehension are important! Copy written inquiries to improve neatness and correct mistakes. You may check out copies of the book.

Earth group: Choose a minimum of *two* projects; *one* must be from List A.

Sky group: Choose a minimum of *three* projects; *one* must be from List A.

Sea group: Choose a minimum of *four* projects; *two* must be from List A.

(Continued)

Figure 8.6 (Continued)

LIST A	LIST B
1. *Describe,* in a well-written paragraph, how Mole meets Ratty at the beginning of the story.	1. *Draw* each of the four main characters using information in the book.
2. *List* the four main characters and write a couple of sentences that describe each one and tell who they are.	2. *Sequence* on a timeline at least six things that happen to Toad in the time from his prison escape to his arrival at Ratty's home. Be creative! Use symbols and decorate with pictures.
3. *Describe,* in a well-written paragraph, the hobbies or fads to which Toad is attracted.	3. *Dramatize* for the class Toad's monologue on page 192 ("Ho, ho, what a clever toad I am ")
4. *Describe,* in two well-written paragraphs, Toad's clever escapes from Toad Hall and prison.	4. *Recite* Toad's song from pages 192 to 193 for the class.
5. *Evaluate* whether Toad is a likable character. In a well-written paragraph, describe some of his faults and gifts, then give your final decision.	5. *Create* a storyboard (separate scenes, as in a comic book) of the series of events that take place in Chapter 5, "Dulce Domum." Write a brief description under each scene.
Make up an inquiry of your own and submit it for approval!	6. *Create* small clay figures of at least two main characters.
	7. *Design* a diorama or triorama of one of the following scenes: • Recovering Toad Hall from the Wild Wooders • The barge woman and Toad on the canal • Toad's escape from prison • Ratty and Mole's picnic in Chapter 1 (don't forget to include the otter!)
	8. *Paint* a scene from the story using watercolors. Write a brief description at the bottom.

Coping With Decision-Making Difficulty

Some students will have difficulty making choices or sticking with their decisions because they have too much input or too many possibilities. Often, they have not had experience with making successful decisions. If students seem to lack confidence in making choices, meet with them briefly after they make choices. Give them feedback and reassurance about the selection. A smile, a comment such as, "That activity seems like it will be so much fun for you!" or a thumbs up may be all they need to feel acknowledged and confident.

Sometimes, students will jump from center to center; they can't seem to stay at one. They may be hyperactive or have other attentional disorders; some students seem to have difficulty sustaining attention for more than about 11 minutes (I've noticed that this is about the same amount of time between commercials during TV shows!). But many students are just curious about what others are doing or need a break every few minutes. I always encourage these students to go scout what others are doing, get a drink, walk around (a little), and then return to the area they have chosen.

When I was in school and was given a chance to choose a project, I always wanted to find out what my friends were doing first. I would be a social butterfly, going around asking the other students what their choices were before I could make my decision. In some cases, I took up most of my work time! If my teacher had said, "Okay, Martha, you have five minutes to discuss with a friend what your choice will be," I know I would have hustled and decided quickly.

The following chapter will provide suggestions about how you can help students develop internal motivation that will help them set reasonable goals. The chapter will also discuss how to encourage students to self-assess their own work, design a generic rubric to assist you as you provide feedback, as well as more suggestions on how you might use these tasks as culminating projects for evaluation.

WHERE TO BEGIN

1. Create choices in homework. Sometimes, it seems overwhelming at first to orchestrate choices for a whole class to make during class time. We are often more willing and able to manage individual choices for homework activities. Determine a short list of projects or activities that might be done at home during the week. Make sure that they all can be done independently and carry, at least in your mind, equal weight or value. Make sure the instructions to the students are clear, and include a cover letter to parents about your plan and expectations.

2. List extension or follow-up activities that could be the culminating projects for a unit of study. Textbooks often include such enrichment activities in the support materials. Make sure students and parents know the expectations and how they will be evaluated. It is important to keep your list short at first and to ensure that the choices are of equal value or require equal effort.

3. If you have been doing centers at the primary level and have had complex rotation schedules, consider having some free choice time. You will need to establish appropriate procedures. Make students accountable for their choices. Perhaps they could share their experiences and choices in a brief gathering after the free choice time.

Additional Sample Book Projects

1. Imagine you are a Hollywood screenwriter. In a one-page writing, describe what story scenes you would film and what scenes you would not film and why.

2. Draw a comic strip of the plot.

3. Create a board game of the plot. Tell how the game relates to the story.

4. Write a one-act play about one important chapter in the book.

5. Select a key scene from the story and create a diorama of it.

6. Draw the main characters on large paper. Include collage pictures and words from magazines to describe the character.

7. Create a crossword puzzle of the characters and main elements of the story.

8. Write a one-page new ending for the story.

9. Perform a puppet or finger-puppet show about one aspect of the story.

10. Write a newspaper-style article as if the story were happening today.

11. Create a mobile of the story. Parts of the mobile will represent various characters or scenes.

12. Develop a filmstrip or create overhead transparencies to tell the story.

13. Create a new design for a book cover. Use the inside flap to write a short summary of the story.

14. Write the essence of the story in a poem.

15. Pantomime the story line for the class.

16. Propose a possible video game that uses the story elements.

17. Paint or sketch at least three key scenes from the story.

18. Compose a rap or song (it's okay to use a common melody) that tells the story.

19. Perform a monologue for the class of something the main character may have been thinking or pondering at some point during the story.

WHAT SHOULD I DO NEXT?

9

Setting Goals and Using Feedback to Reach Success

Self-Assessment and Learning Celebrations

When students have opportunities to make choices, have access to timely feedback to monitor their progress, and are able to reach their goals through their own efforts, their brains' natural dopamine reward systems will activate. Orchestrating metacognitive strategies helps learners understand their brains' learning preferences and strengths. When students are provided opportunities to make choices, they begin to set their own learning goals. They are thinking for themselves and developing self-determination—the opposite of *learned helplessness!* A positive emotional climate and a low-stress environment allow the brain to internalize feedback and stay focused on goals. As students begin to know their own personal strengths and challenges, they can make better choices and set realistic goals.

In brain-compatible, learner-centered classrooms, students learn how to

- Set reasonable long- and short-term goals,
- Analyze tasks to determine the skills and resources that will be needed,
- Make personally meaningful choices,
- Identify their most developed multiple intelligences and learning styles,
- Seek out feedback and self-assess progress, and
- Reflect on the learning process and use metacognitive strategies.

Setting and Achieving Goals

You can develop the following strategies to assist students in setting and achieving academic and personal goals. If you implement this system routinely in your classroom, students will begin to store it as a program that they can count on to succeed in the future.

1. **Know and understand the plan or task through agendas, schedules, and assigned projects.** Students shouldn't have to be mind readers. Even to begin to set goals, students

must clearly understand the expectations, timelines, and challenges involved.

- Post and review a daily agenda, and review it at the beginning of class to alert students to the tasks they are going to do on that day and in what order.
- Write up clear expectations and requirements for projects and homework assignments. If possible, send copies home to parents.
- Post procedures for tasks and review them before starting a project.
- Post, or send home, calendars that clearly mark events, deadlines, and benchmarks for extended projects.
- At independent centers, post the tasks and expectations in writing, or identify them with symbols, so all students understand the goals.

2. **Note personal relevance and connection to the curriculum content or task.** Students should have an opportunity to discover what meaning the task or curriculum selection has for them. Although the course description and you will often determine the content of the class, students should be able to see how they can align their own needs, wants, and experiences with the instructional goals. You can often achieve this end by offering them an opportunity to choose how they can achieve the goal (the process or product).

- Introduce the instructional goal in a way that shows students it is personally relevant to them: link it to the here and now, relate it to their personal and social concerns, or tie it to their prior experiences.
- Assist students by generating an emotional bridge from their world and daily lives to the academic task. This connection can help students generate personal feelings about the topic.
- Ensure students understand that there will be opportunities to choose topics and projects within the instructional goals. Students may be able to choose extension activities, areas in which to become experts, or ways they will be assessed.

3. **Create opportunities and develop students' abilities to analyze tasks and make plans.** Once they know a task, students need guidance in analyzing it. By analyzing the steps they need to complete successfully, the students create a game plan that includes a timeline and benchmarks.

  - As part of the initial lesson, facilitate a discussion about the sequence of steps students need to complete the task.
  - Help students visualize what the task might look like at various benchmarks along the way.
  - Teach students how to predict and estimate the amount of time each step will take. Plot these times on a calendar or daily schedule.
  - Begin to develop rubrics or self-assessment surveys that help students evaluate their progress. Ask students to reflect on what a good one looks like.

4. **Determine what resources students need to complete the task.** Assess the materials you have and plan to acquire necessary items you don't have. In a truly enriched environment, many of the resources are available to students, depending, of course, on students' ages and degree of responsibility, as well as the level of support available from home.

  - Students note the supplies or resources available in the classroom or the library.
  - Students will use various ways to get the materials they need outside the classroom.
  - If possible, allow students to have access to the Internet, and train them in the skills necessary to gather information there.

5. **Give students accurate, timely feedback throughout the task.** Their peers, you, other adults, and the students themselves can give feedback. The final evaluation should not surprise students. If you have been giving accurate feedback at several points, then students will be aware of the degree of success with which they have completed the task.

  - Set up logical points within the process to give feedback (formative assessments). These benchmarks will probably be the same for all students. At these sessions, compliment students on what is developing well and give them constructive comments about the areas that need to improve.

- Creating a system for giving feedback is helpful. Develop a rubric for the final evaluation (summative assessment), and use it during the project to assess progress as well.

- Clearly define and delineate the evaluation tools to students before the final assessment. This measure allows students to practice self-assessment before they submit any work for feedback.

- It is your responsibility to create a system that provides timely, even immediate, feedback. One way to ensure timely feedback is to assess different benchmarks on different days. Rotate days on which the groups hand in their work.

- Make the feedback system multidynamic. In other words, you might ask students to do a self-assessment first, then get feedback from two peers, then submit the revised work to you.

6. **Allow reflection time for students to create new meaning and gain understanding.** This personal process time can allow for new understandings to sink in and for what Candace Pert (1999) refers to as "self-honesty." Students can use the time for reflection to consider possible modifications to their work. This also allows for what is known as "the spacing effect." First written about 120 years ago, this theory suggests that "cramming" (intense, last-minute studying) the night before an exam will not be as effective as more frequent study sessions over a much longer span of time. The brain needs a chance to process new information in order to "file" it into long-term memory. Short intervals of time between the acquisition of new learning will allow the brain to reflect on the new information. To invoke an emotional connection to the work, give students the opportunity to discuss the process and the feedback with others in a peer-review group.

- Just because something seems relevant to you doesn't mean that students will see personal connections immediately. Permit personal process time to allow students to link the task to prior learning and patterns.
- Take time to honor the work students have done and the goods things that are emerging. When you immediately suggest changes, you don't take time to recognize and allow students to savor the points they have done well.
- Ask students to restate feedback in their own words, writing it in a journal to help them clarify and process the comments.

Meaningful Feedback as Acknowledgment

To acknowledge our achievements and effort, we seek feedback from several sources and in several ways. The hardest part of all the techniques is allowing for the time! In school, it is so easy to push the time limit to the very end of class and simply *nct* have the time to process, reflect, and give feedback. We really should begin to consider feedback time as the key point of the whole lesson.

Interaction, Process, or Experience

If you design learning activities to include real experiences, there will be lots of opportunities for immediate feedback. As students do experiments or discovery play or attempt to solve problems, the reactions and effects they observe while doing the activity will provide ample feedback. Trial and error is extremely motivating to someone who is working on a task.

Give students many opportunities to have experiences that teach and reward through the experience itself. In primary classrooms, set up choice centers to encourage building, creating, sewing, computing. These activities provide daily opportunities for children to find out how things work. Getting to build with blocks or Legos gives students immediate feedback: If something doesn't look the way they want it to or falls over, then students have to keep trying to get it right, which motivates them. When they complete a project, they have a real sense of accomplishment. In intermediate classrooms, allow students to work with similar items that are more age appropriate. They might create electric circuits to light bulbs and make bells go off or build an irrigation system for the class garden. If students get stuck, they may ask for some adult feedback, but more often than not, you will find students deeply focused on something they are trying to figure out, making modifications and forging onward.

I remember a time when my students were working on creating solar cookers out of pizza boxes. They had to create an insulated oven, cover the surface with smooth aluminum foil, then design a way to adjust the reflective surface so it heated the cooking area. We went through a lot of foil, masking tape, string, and cardboard that day, but the various completed designs were incredible. The adult leaders gave the students very little feedback. The students understood the concepts and had the resources and time they needed. Their level of concentration and motivation was extremely high. And quite honestly, the lukewarm hot dogs and quesadillas with only slightly melted cheese never tasted any better than they did that day!

Technology: The "Immediate Feedback" Express

Although I tend to resist allowing students to work on computers for routine tasks that they can do with other materials at school, there is no denying that through technology students are able to receive immediate feedback. Even a conscientious well-organized teacher couldn't provide the incredible step-by-step, task-by-task guidance that a well-designed computer program can.

If at First You Don't Succeed . . .
The Power of "Do-Overs"

Try it again! We are so encouraging to young children as they learn how to walk, talk, tie their shoes, dance, play a sport, learn a musical instrument, and so on. If they make a mistake, we quickly give them an opportunity to do it again. They get a free pass to try and get it right! We know this to be the natural way one learns. On the playground when someone has difficulty doing something or there is a controversial play, students will ask for a "do-over." What happened to this encouragement to persevere and opportunities to redo tasks in classrooms? Often, students are evaluated and graded the *first* time they are actually trying something new. How unfair!

I am a proponent of do-overs during the learning process. I believe that students need second and third chances to try new things. During the process of learning, the brain will reorganize the neural connections based on successes *and* mistakes. This is a powerful form of immediate relevant feedback. Given a non-judgmental environment, the learner becomes more creative and perseveres.

Scientific discoveries and medical breakthroughs would be stagnant if laboratory do-overs weren't the norm for research studies. In fact, in science experimentation, "discrepant events" (unexpected results) are actually more interesting than what had been predicted. In other words, it might be more useful and interesting to see what curious result had occurred rather than to be unimpressed with the predictable outcome. What if we celebrated creative attempts with learners? No consequences for incorrect responses, just a new learning opportunity.

If a student has given an assignment or task a try but isn't successful or correct, I encourage (or insist) that they take a do-over. Before they begin again, I ask them to reflect and verbalize what they are going to do differently on this next attempt. I don't ask them what they did wrong. I understand that every time that the learner's brain is forced to recall the incorrect process, it will only strengthen that brain connection. I don't want the brain to remember the wrong way of doing something. I would rather the learner analyze and predict the correct way they will complete the task when given the chance for the do-over. "Inside the brain, neural networks become more efficient when a learner tries out several possible options and eliminates the ones that don't work. Feedback-driven learning makes more accurate and complex connections" (Jensen, 2005, p. 53).

Self-Reflection

As we help students learn how to gather feedback, we can model for them how to self-reflect. Something as simple as reviewing the daily agenda at the end of the day and noting which items you completed and which ones need more time can show them how to self-reflect. Occasionally, I have reviewed some of their work and decided to modify a strategy or lesson I was using. I always share such decisions with them, so they know I constantly look at my own work as a teacher, just as I want them to look at theirs as students. Tell them when you are noting what goes on around you and reflecting on decisions or modifications.

I think the greatest reason students don't know how to self-reflect is that we haven't given them time to do so and to process their experiences. It is during this mental rehearsal and reflection that greater understanding can occur. An excellent way for students to begin self-reflection is by keeping journals. After they complete an activity or at points during the process, ask them to write a little in their journals. Provide some frame sentences, such as those that follow, as writing prompts.

- I think this project is going well because . . .
- The hardest part of this work was . . .
- If I do this kind of activity again, I think I will . . .
- The thing I wish I knew before I started was . . .
- If I were going to show this to someone, I would share it with _____ because . . .

As I said in the previous chapter, give students access to any assessment criteria you are using, such as a copy of a rubric. If they have the information in advance, they can determine whether they are meeting the criteria at the desired level.

Feedback From Peers

In a learner-centered classroom, the trusting relationships that are formed will be the foundation for peer feedback. Remember that we usually aren't willing to hear ideas or be influenced by someone with whom we have no relationship or sense of trust. Set up procedures so that peers can safely give each other accurate, meaningful feedback.

The easiest way to start peer feedback is by assigning partners. Students pair with other students whom they already know and trust. They share writings or drawings that they have completed and ask partners to give them two compliments and one suggestion. I usually call this process "one to grow on." When students give feedback about stories and creative writing, give them a specific framework for the type of critique they are doing. For instance, when they read the story, are they supposed to be checking spelling or just noting if it makes sense? Maybe they are just supposed to give feedback about whether or not the author's name is on the paper, the pages are in order, and stapled together. Be sure they know, so they don't waste time or fail to do what you want them to do.

You'll already have various groups set up in the classroom; there will be many other opportunities for students to get peer responses. Encourage table teams to give feedback. In their writing workshops, they can get feedback, editing assistance, and encouragement about stories they are writing.

Another good method for introducing students to peer feedback is to have some students serve as peer tutors or classroom experts. If some students have already mastered certain tasks or concepts, tell other students who they are; those who need help can ask them for feedback. This process saves you a lot of time, as well, because students don't see you as the only expert in the classroom. I post a sign in my room that says

Ask three, then me!

to remind students to ask three of their peers, then me if they still don't have helpful feedback.

It is your job to model what respectful, accurate, meaningful feedback looks and sounds like. It is also your job to help students as they learn how to deliver constructive criticism. I provide students with a list of "Socratic questions" and statements that they can also use to generate a greater understanding of someone's work, presentation, or ideas (see Figure 9.1).

Figure 9.1

Socratic Questions

- What examples can you give to show what you mean here?
- I wonder if what you are saying is . . .
- What is your reason for saying that?
- Help me understand what you mean here.
- Could you clarify that comment?
- Why do you believe that?
- How do you know that?

We can also model and note for students when we, as teachers, seek feedback for ourselves. At the end of lessons or activities, I will gather the students together and ask them, "What did you like?" "What parts of the lesson worked well?" "What aspects of the lesson do you think I need to change for next time?"

Feedback From Teachers or Other Experts

It is often difficult to create ways for us to give meaningful, immediate feedback to all students on a regular basis. We know that often the simplest response from us can go a long way. Many students just need brief acknowledgment and encouragement to keep them going. In reality, only a few might be able to tolerate a long feedback session. In fact, a stressed learner, especially if in a survival response mode, will prefer feedback after she has calmed down.

But one key aspect of teacher feedback is that it should happen while the student is working on a project or a task so the student still has time to modify the product based on the new information. Nothing is more frustrating than finishing a project and finding out that you were off base right from the beginning. If students get feedback only in the form of an evaluation at the end of a project, they may not find it meaningful; they might just look at the grade and are likely to forget whatever you said for the next time. As you rotate during a work period, give feedback to several students. Use words and written comments. Or, you can often ask a table group to leave work out on their desks one afternoon each week so you have only five or six students' work to respond to. I try to have small groups rotate to work with me every day so that I have the opportunity to check in and redirect them, if necessary.

Written Feedback

When conducting miniconferences with students about something they are doing on paper, ask permission to write on their work before you make marks or comments. Ask them to attach that copy to whatever final work they turn in so that you can note the improvements and changes. Older children can write the feedback and corrections themselves. Hand them your "fancy pen" with which to do it, and they will feel an extra sense of acknowledgment and affirmation.

Score as You Go

When reviewing students' work, such as responses to questions or math problems and computations, if an answer is correct, mark it immediately. My colleague Robert Ellingsen is a master at this. As students ask for help or feedback, he draws a star or smile on everything correct he sees or all the parts that are going well. The students know immediately that they have been successful, they feel an immediate sense of accomplishment, and they are motivated to continue with the rest of the assignment. Also, he doesn't have a stack of work because, when students turn in their papers, a large part of their work has already been evaluated.

Work Folders

For many activities, ask students to bring or create folders to hold their works in progress. We often create a response chart that we attach to the front of the folders. On the chart are lines where I put the date and a comment along with my initials. The chart serves as a record sheet for any work that I am reviewing. I also encourage students to take the folders home and ask their parents to indicate that they reviewed the work with their children.

An easy way to make a folder is to use a 9-by-12–inch manila envelope. Lift up the flap on the back side. Cut down each of the side edges about two inches and fold the clasp edge into the folder. Moisten the flap, fold it down, and seal it to the exposed top. The students write their names in large letters on the flap. The envelope is now a nifty pocket folder to keep papers in and pass in for a check.

Talk It Out

Although you may often be rushed and give quick feedback, be sure to allow students time to explain what they are doing. Be sure to ask them to talk themselves through their thinking. This strategy is a perfect way to help them learn self-reflection skills. Although they might think that the ideas are coming from you, be sure to point out the ways in which they are thinking for themselves!

Rotate Feedback

To keep from being overwhelmed with student work that needs feedback, rotate which group you work with each day. I found this method especially helpful when I wanted to respond to them in their journals. I would do one table team each day. The groups knew which day of the week to leave their folders or journals on their desks. I was able to respond to everyone at least once a week.

Verbal and Nonverbal

Don't forget how powerful and important nonverbal gestures and quick verbal affirmations can be! I use high-fives and knuckle-bumps often, and the students helped me create a plethora of variations on the basic hand slap! I would occasionally put my hands on a student's head to perform a "Vulcan Mind-Transfer" that I had invented. It meant that this student was being so smart that I wanted to get some of the intelligence transferred to my own brain. Use a simple thumbs-up sign from across a room.

When giving quick verbal feedback, don't overuse praise statements such as "good," "super," "okay," "better!" and "well done!" I create my own statements, smile, and make eye contact when I say them; what a great affirmation for students. "Now you're cooking!" "I can see you are really getting into this!" "This is blowing me away!" "I don't think I've ever seen anything like this!" "Did you do this? Wow!" *"I'm impressed!"*

You can offer even constructive criticism or a little nudge in short humorous statements that convey your suggestion: "Is this your personal best today?" "I was wondering what you've been up to." "Hmm, so you must be really thinking about what you're doing over the weekend, huh?" "I wonder what else is on your mind today?" "Do you think you can spare a little more energy to finish this correctly?"

Orchestrating ways for students to receive constructive feedback in a timely way is challenging. Different subjects and various grade levels have unique needs when it comes to feedback. *How to Give Effective Feedback to Your Students* by Susan M. Brookhart (2008) provides tons of examples of good strategies to use with a variety of students.

> Good feedback gives students information they need so they can understand where they are in their learning and what to do next—the cognitive factor. Once they feel they understand what to do and why, most students develop a feeling that they have control over their own learning—the motivational factor. (Brookhart, 2008, p. 3)

Self-Assessment

There are several ways to encourage students to self-assess their work, their behavior, their attitudes, their participation, their own understandings. They can self-reflect through journal writing, essays, group sharing, rubrics, and surveys. Younger children can use pictures to demonstrate ways in which they participated, what something looked like for them, and what they were doing during the task.

Journals

I encourage all students to keep learning-reflection journals. In the journals, they do quick writings that give them a chance to process experiences and articulate goals. I prefer that they share the journal with me occasionally, so if students want to keep a private diary or journal, they do it in addition to their learning-reflection journal.

I asked my students to copy the daily agenda in their daily logs when they arrived. After they noted the tasks we would be working on, I asked them to write one or two goals for the day underneath the agenda. At the end of the day, they would go back to the agenda and check off the things they had completed and note which items they needed to finish. Then they assessed how well they had met their goals for the day and wrote a comment underneath.

Small Process Groups

Often, students can gather in groups of three to six to share their work and offer feedback to one another. The groups can be set up to give formal feedback for writing or peer response. You can also have table teams or randomly selected groups. Establish procedures for sharing, listening, and giving feedback. Group members use a rubric to guide their suggestions. Students then take the feedback and reflect either in their journals or by telling the group how they will use the information.

Surveys

Sometimes I have used a checklist survey to help students self-assess. The questions help them reflect on their progress and consider what still needs to be done. A good self-survey encourages students to reflect on how well they have participated in a group's process and progress. The example in Figure 9.2 allows students to self-assess effectively.

Figure 9.2

Team Member Survey

Respond to each item: + = Most of the time, " = Some of the time, – = Not very much

- I felt included in the group; I felt the other members listened to me.
- I voiced my opinions on issues and shared my ideas.
- I accepted the various ideas and opinions that my teammates shared.
- I accepted some of the responsibilities of the group; I did my share.
- I shared materials with my group.
- I completed my tasks on time; no one had to bug me to get done.
- My teammates appreciated my efforts and thought I contributed.
- I told others when I thought they were doing a good job; I complimented them.
- I tried to resolve conflicts as they came up; I did not escalate problems.
- My teammates feel that they can trust me; I show them respect.

Rubrics

Share any rubrics or evaluation criteria with students at the onset of a task or project. This tool allows students to do the most effective self-evaluations. Rubrics have several criteria that might include content, process, mechanics, timeliness, presentation, artistic quality, and creativity (see a sample on opposite page). A three-point gradient will probably give younger children sufficient feedback. The middle level or number two would indicate what a basic project should look or be like. A number one would indicate that elements were missing. A number three would indicate that the project or task had all aspects completed correctly; it went beyond the original expectations.

Older students and adults seem to do better with four- or five-point rubrics. When writing the indicators for success, I always find it easiest to write the first level—that is, what an incomplete task would look like—and what the highest level would look like (see example in Figure 9.3). I complete the indicators in between later. I will often give students the indicators for the second-highest level only, then let them be creative in coming up with what an exceptional product would look like or be like.

Figure 9.3

Multi-Dynamic Project Rubric				
Assessment Area	*Awesome!* 4	*A Good Effort!* 3	*A Work in Progress* 2	*Just Beginning* 1
Organization	• Extremely well organized • Easy to follow • Flows smoothly	• Some organization • Most ideas flowed • Thoughtful arrangement • Occasional confusion	• Somewhat unorganized • No flow of ideas • Scattered • Lost reader	• Confusing • Difficult to follow • Lacked format
Content Accuracy and Understanding	• Comprehensive and accurate facts • Detailed explanations • Added to reader's understanding	• Most facts accurate • A few errors in information • Some explanations not clearly developed	• Somewhat accurate • Several errors in information • Content not researched • Inconsistent explanations	• Ideas not coherent • Most facts not accurate or researched • Based on assumed information; misleading
Comprehensive Research	• Went above and beyond to research • Used Internet effectively • Used six or more resources	• Utilized a variety of resources • Did research out of class • Used four or more resources	• Used most of the resources provided in an acceptable manner • No evidence of consulting outside resources	• Ineffective use of resources • Did little or no research • No evidence of research
Presentation and Mechanics	• Ideas presented in a unique manner • Impeccable mechanics • Engaging	• Ideas presented in an effective manner • A few mechanical errors	• At times, some ideas presented clearly • Many mechanical errors • Seemed in draft form rather than final	• Lacked effective presentation qualities • Ideas unclear • Serious mechanical errors

(Continued)

Figure 9.3 (Continued)

Multi-Dynamic Project Rubric				
Assessment Area	Awesome! 4	A Good Effort! 3	A Work in Progress 2	Just Beginning 1
Creativity	• Clever and unique • Original ideas enhanced total project • Artwork and other elements added a great deal of interest	• Thoughtfully presented • Artwork and other elements added interest	• Few original touches to enhance project • Basic artwork and other elements • Obviously didn't spend time developing	• First draft quality • Predictable • Just covered the basics • No artwork or other elements to add interest

Understanding Your Learning Preferences

Multiple Intelligences

Most teachers have at least heard about Howard Gardner's (1983) multiple intelligence theory. In his search for a better way to determine human intellectual capacities, Gardner defined *intelligence* as

> a set of skills of problem solving—enabling the individual to resolve genuine problems or difficulties that he or she encounters and, when appropriate, to create an effective product—and must also entail the potential for *finding or creating* problems—thereby laying the groundwork for the acquisition of new knowledge. (pp. 60–61)

Understanding their multiple intelligences can help students set goals and self-assess. I strongly recommend that you give all students a foundation in the theory and the language of the intelligences. Even primary students can begin to understand the concepts and competencies associated with each of the intelligences. Many teachers have set up classroom centers named for the intelligences, such as the "Linguistic Station" or "Word-Smart Center."

I think Thomas Armstrong (1999, 2000, 2009), David Lazear (1999), and Spencer Kagan (1998) offer the best resources for understanding and implementing multiple intelligences. See Armstrong's revised and updated *Seven Kinds of Smart + 2* (1999), *Multiple Intelligences in the Classroom* (2009), and *In Their Own Way* (2000). Kagan's comprehensive guide is titled *Multiple Intelligences: The Complete MI Book.* Understanding the various intelligences and their implications for teaching and learning is an important step teachers must take to effectively differentiate instruction.

As students begin to understand their own natural strengths, they will know why they are drawn to certain types of activities and projects. They will also begin to understand why some tasks seem so challenging. In most cases, students find tasks demanding that require them to use an intelligence they have not yet developed. By understanding their areas of expertise, students will be able to select activities and set learning goals that they are more likely to meet. When assigned a challenging task, students may discover ways they can utilize personal strengths to succeed. Mastering multiplication facts, for example, may be easier for bodily-kinesthetic learners if they can jump rope or dance while memorizing.

I use a self-assessment survey to help students see which intelligences they seem to be developing and which ones they have *not* yet developed. I do not survey them to label them, or to determine what they can and can't do. The checklist is only a survey that may identify current strengths. By knowing these strengths, they can more confidently set goals and make choices.

I know, for example, that I have very strong interpersonal and bodily-kinesthetic intelligences. If given choices of ways to complete a task, I always choose working with others and creating a presentation or performance. By making that choice, I increase the likelihood of my success, based on my past experiences and my understanding of my own intelligences.

Give the checklists on pages 222–226 ("Life Skills for Success" and "Eight Kinds of Smart") to your students to use as a self-assessment. The 10 statements for each of the intelligences are written from a child's perspective. Many more indicators exist. Send the survey home with younger students, and ask their parents to assist them in reading and responding. Remember that there isn't a final score in each area. In fact, it is important to remember that marking as many as 4 or 5 out of 10 items under each of the intelligences could indicate your flexibility and aptitude for using all intelligences. You are not limited in any way! Have students use the record sheet to create a bar graph. One will easily be able to identify which intelligences are already well developed and which intelligences you have yet to develop.

Authentic Achievement

Humans consistently seek new experiences and are curious without needing external rewards. The brain begins to produce pleasurable feelings when accomplishing a task, enjoying an activity, succeeding, sharing affection, laughing, or being entertained. The brain self-satisfies by seeking out novelty and challenge. If students are in a threatening environment, then the brain releases chemicals such as cortisol, adrenaline, and vasopressin, which generate a survival response and possible anger and aggression. In brain-compatible, learner-centered classrooms, orchestrate opportunities for the brain to generate intrinsic motivation. Provide ample feedback and acknowledgment, and celebrate learning; rely less on external rewards and motivators.

Creating a Culture for Success

Do your students experience personal success every day? Do they observe others, including you, being successful? Do they routinely celebrate their successes and those of others? Does the climate in your learning environment exude an "I can do it!" feeling? Your answers to these questions will indicate whether you have fostered a positive climate and a culture that emphasizes success.

As a teacher, I try to create and facilitate a culture of success in the classroom. My own positive attitude and ability to handle daily stress will be a key factor in setting the tone. Without being too much of a Pollyanna, I always point out the positive aspects of situations. My students know and understand the saying "Is your glass half full or half empty?"

I recognized this same attitude and encouragement when I was on the television game show *Hollywood Squares* years ago. I noticed that whenever contestants made obviously ridiculous or thoughtless moves on the giant board, the charismatic host Peter Marshall wouldn't humiliate them or call attention to their blunder. He would simply say, in a matter-of-fact way, "Well, this may work out." And, incredibly, it often did! Just for the record, he never had to say it to me. I was on a nighttime version and won more than $4,000 in cash and prizes, including a trip to England. I missed the car by one question. Well, I guess that part didn't work out.

In a positive environment, you can foster a culture of success. In such a culture, students have positive self-concepts and self-esteem. They know, from a pattern of experiences, that even if at first they don't achieve a goal, they will be encouraged and given an opportunity to try again until they succeed. They also know that learning is a process through which they will construct their own understandings in multiple attempts and modifications. When people succeed immediately on every task they attempt, they are not challenged and their motivation may wane.

Weaning Off Rewards

To establish brain-compatible learning environments, we must wean our students off rewards and outright bribery! While I used to think upper-grade students were the only ones trained to expect rewards, I now realize that our kindergarten students arrive already programmed into working and performing for extrinsic rewards. Obviously, many parents give rewards. But the pattern worsens in school, perhaps simply with stars and stickers in primary classrooms. As kids get a little older, it seems to grow into pizza parties and privileges. By middle school, the stakes get higher, and parents continue to fall into the trap by giving monetary rewards for grades. Children and many adults are terribly dependent on what compensation they will receive for their compliance or performance. But internal motivation decreases as the drive for external rewards increases.

Studies have shown that providing a tangible reward may cause the learners to change their behavior or do something to get the reward; when the reward is gone, they revert back to the old behavior. As Alfie Kohn (2006) describes reward systems, they do not promote meaningful learning or intrinsic motivation: "Rewards, like punishments, can only manipulate someone's actions. They do nothing to help a child become a kind or caring person" (p. 34).

Occasionally, it's okay to offer incentives for short-term compliance, for instance, if we need to get something done quickly. On a day-to-day basis, though, we must provide only acknowledgment and recognition for students' efforts and successes. We also need to orchestrate learning celebrations that include parents. These family gatherings will provide the emotional and social recognition that students can use to affirm their efforts and success.

> Although rewards are a fact of life, the time has come in education when the wholesale bribery system of giving out endless supplies of stickers, candies, and other tangibles has got to come to a halt. Let's stop the "What's in it for me?" welfare and bribery system. The best reward is the satisfaction of a job well done. (Wong & Wong, 2005, p. 160)

Take some time to discuss with students why you are gradually phasing out the reward systems and what your new expectations are. Then allow reward systems you have used to gradually disappear. For instance, many students are "addicted" to stamps or stickers on their written work and papers. When I finally decided not to put stars on their pages, I created a *self-serve station*. The station was a small metal box that had all the miscellaneous stickers and stamps I had collected. If students felt that they deserved a visual reward when they got a paper back, they could go choose one and put it on for themselves. This replacement method served many purposes:

- Students looked a little harder at the comments from me on their work to see if they should have a sticker.

- Within weeks, the box was almost forgotten, with only a few students still going to it regularly. The stickers from the box seemed to have become unnecessary and time consuming.
- Eventually, only those students who recognized that their piece of work was an exceptional effort or performance went and put on their own form of acknowledgment and affirmation. They were in transition!

Recognizing Student Effort and Authentic Achievement

Learner-centered classrooms will be noticeably different in many ways. The formative and summative assessments will include many types of products and performances along with the more traditional methods. Designing genuine activities for the students to complete will increase their motivation and the meaning they find in their learning. Instead of giving tasks that go nowhere, that nobody sees, and that the student doesn't value, provide summative assessments on tasks that are authentic, that require the students to do something logical, and that arise from the knowledge itself. For example, ask students to build something, design brochures and newsletters, write press releases, paint murals, provide community service, design posters, orchestrate a celebration, create a museum of artwork or projects, send letters to corporations, invent something, plant and maintain a garden, clean up a river—the list is endless.

When students complete these types of projects, you may or may not evaluate their final efforts. You should, however, take regular opportunities to recognize their efforts through assemblies, achievement certificates, news releases, school newsletters, photograph displays, or even simple words of appreciation at a classroom gathering. Students will appreciate the recognition, but they will have already had the feedback to know in their minds and hearts how meaningful and successful they have been. This additional acknowledgment is meant to honor them, thank them, and provide an opportunity to inspire others to produce the types of projects their peers are doing. It can build an awareness of the depth of someone's involvement and commitment that the class may not otherwise have known about.

Impromptu Recognition

You can plan an event to recognize someone's efforts, success, or achievements. But the more common and easiest recognition to orchestrate is impromptu. During a work period, perhaps you notice three students working very hard, above and beyond the call of duty. Before dismissing for recess, take a moment to ask them to stand or simply put your hand on their shoulders and publicly make a short statement about their degree of work and success. Some classes might spontaneously applaud or snap their fingers. Lately, I've seen students imitate the way you honor musicians and celebrities, by pushing palms upward in the air several times, as if they were raising the roof, "givin' props." A great high five or knuckle-bump in front of the class can go a long way, too.

You might try something other than public commendation for a consistently good effort or a spontaneous change of behavior and cooperation. I often invite students to eat lunch with me. Even older students find it a real treat. Of course, we don't just eat lunch! We put on some of their favorite pop music, and I always have something for a special dessert, usually juice ice pops kept in the staff refrigerator. Look for special efforts or adjustments in behavior, and once a week or so, invite a few students to lunch. You can ensure that all students will get the opportunity.

I have had a few students who didn't understand why other students were getting to have lunch with me. I took the opportunity to point out exactly what I thought the students' efforts were and the qualities I thought they had demonstrated. Eventually some of the students who didn't understand at first would point out to me when they were "being good"! Awareness of what behavior would gain my appreciation and recognition was just beginning for these students.

Achievement Awards

A certificate, ribbon, or award of some kind can be a treasured lifetime keepsake. I know I still have a box full of tokens I received while in school. In a learner-centered classroom, you'll begin to phase out many competitive events, such as math races, spelling bees, poetry contests, athletic competitions, and science fairs. While many students enjoy the external motivators these types of events create, such activities usually have the same students winning all the time, with *a lot* of "losers." If students aren't gifted in a particular area, there isn't a chance for them ever to be acknowledged, even if they are making great progress. You should note the efforts even of those students who are not at the top of the class.

Regular, frequent recognition ceremonies can be a way to pay public acknowledgement to students who have been successful and are gaining ground in certain areas. A simple certificate, signed and dated by a respected adult, given with a handshake in a public forum, is a special event for many students (and parents)! Determining descriptors for the awards will be the key. Rather than a generic math award, perhaps recognize someone's achievement in problem solving, effort, or analysis. Instead of certificates for spelling, consider certificates for achievement in accuracy, communication skills, or perseverance. The life skills for success described in the next section are a terrific resource for the types of skills, behaviors, and competencies for which we would like to give achievement awards to our students.

Life Skills for Success

In the midst of the controversy about whether or not schools should teach values of any kind, Dorothy Rich (1988) published *MegaSkills: How Families Can Help Children Succeed in School and*

Beyond. The book sent a powerful message to parents and educators about the skills beyond the three Rs that all children need to be successful beyond school: "MegaSkills are the very basic values, attitudes, and behaviors that determine a child's achievements" (back cover). The set of top 10 skills that Rich recommends includes confidence, motivation, effort, responsibility, initiative, perseverance, caring, teamwork, common sense, and problem solving.

In 1992, Thomas Lickona, a well-known psychologist and religious educator, published *Educating for Character: How Our Schools Can Teach Respect and Responsibility,* in which he echoes what Rich and others continue to say: Teaching very basic life skills to our children is *everyone's* responsibility, and doing so is necessary to ensure that we build a decent, humane society. In 1997, members of the research and guidelines committee of the Collaborative for the Advancement of Social and Emotional Learning (CASEL) at the University of Illinois wrote *Promoting Social and Emotional Learning: Guidelines for Educators.* CASEL's whole purpose is "to support schools and families in their efforts to educate knowledgeable, responsible, and caring young people who will become productive workers and contributing citizens in the twenty-first century" (p. viii). Obviously, many believe that teaching students life skills is vital.

We can and should teach life skills in learner-centered classrooms through orchestrated lessons and activities; teaching them also means noting and recognizing through awards and celebrations our students who exhibit them. While such a list is never finite, I have assimilated various lists into a generic list of skills, values, attitudes, and behaviors to serve us in the classroom as a set of guidelines (see page 222). *Respect* and *responsibility* need to be at the top of the list. The remaining skills can arguably be placed in any order, as long as they are not presented as a hierarchy.

Schoolwide Programs

Many schools have created programs that recognize students who demonstrate the life skills for success. Some have an assembly once a month to honor students whom teachers have nominated because they have consistently or recently demonstrated the skill that was being emphasized that month. Often, a school counselor, vice principal, or an activities director organizes the selected skills for the whole year. In the first month of school, they might emphasize friendship, initiative, or motivation. During December, before the winter vacation, schools often emphasize kindness, citizenship, cooperation, and peace, and encourage community service and family connections. At the end of the school year, they might find that perseverance, sense of humor, and self-control are the most relevant! By dividing the skills over the school year, teachers can select two to four students each month who deserve recognition and acknowledgment in that area. By the end of the year, *all* students will have received a certificate in at least one awards assembly.

Some teachers worry that there may not be a category for the students who present a challenge. I always find that there is at least *one* month (or one life skill) in which students show their talents or expertise. It often becomes the skills in which they are most naturally talented, perhaps those that have landed them in trouble a few times, such as sense of humor, creativity, or curiosity. (I know this because my two sons seem to often fall into these categories!)

Learning Celebrations

When students work hard to create authentic achievements, they are eager to have friends and family view their efforts and help celebrate their work. At the end of in-depth thematic units, I orchestrate a culminating event, performance, or family gathering that marks the unit and gives students public acknowledgment for their efforts.

Culminating Events

Usually, I envision a possible culminating event first; it helps me orchestrate the whole unit, including project choices and the assessment activity. Any activity that publicly showcases student work and effort can serve as a culminating event to celebrate learning.

Possible Culminating Events

- Information fairs
- Museums
- Art shows
- Plays
- How-to stations
- Armchair travel trips
- Miniature workshops
- Invention conventions
- Learning expos
- Discovery exploratorium

As I noted earlier, one of the more popular types of learning celebrations in my intermediate multiage class was a fair. The marine mammal fair was a terrific example of multiage teams of students working together to create a booth, brochures, items to sell, information packets, logos, and drawings of a marine mammal that they had selected for their in-depth study. The intense activity and commitment from students builds almost into a frenzy of learning and production in the days before the event. You know students are hooked when they ask to stay after school to work on stuff, or arrange to go over to others' homes on weekends to work on the booth. I am always reminded of old Andy Hardy movies with Mickey Rooney and Judy Garland. My students seem just as inspired, like they are putting on a "show in the barn"! (I date myself with this reference!)

Other popular events are museums and exploratoriums. At these events, the students have usually created products or works of art to display. They rehearse and serve as docents at the museum, giving short, informative tours. We have had interactive stations, and students have occasionally charged visiting parents a quarter to learn how to do the skill or the activity. Who wouldn't want to pay a quarter to learn how to shake cream in a glass jar to make butter?

Performances

I highly recommend putting on a short play each year. Perhaps it's my own love of the theater and performance, but I know that most children love an opportunity to at least be a part of a play or musical performance. I try to select short plays that have something to do with the topics we are studying. You can shorten longer plays, but narrate parts to link the action together. Your students can adapt many stories and novels to the theater. Make sure everyone is involved in some way: costumes, props, sets, programs, and tickets (even if you don't charge for it!). As the performance date nears, rehearsal will take up more and more class time. Be prepared and remember that the skills the students learn and experience may be more than you can teach them for the whole year.

The experience of performing in front of parents and the community is a memorable one that will last students a lifetime.

The applause, recognition, laughter, mistakes, exhaustion—all of it—constitute feedback that their brains will thrive on. As in many other experiences, the process is the point. The process involved in organizing student performances is incredible, and the final product can be incredibly rewarding.

Family Gatherings

At least three times a year, I organize a family gathering that may or may not also be a learning celebration. At the beginning of school, even before an official back-to-school night, I encourage teachers and some helpful parents to organize a potluck, a burrito bash, a barbecue, or a dessert-a-thon. At these events, my only real expectation is that families have a chance to get to know one another. It is often the first time that children can introduce their friends to their parents. I encourage *both* parents in divorced situations to come and get to know other families who are perhaps in similar circumstances.

There's no question that these events will always be above and beyond the call of our duties as the students' teacher. I have always felt that the extra effort needed to organize them only contributed to my abilities to communicate with parents and my overall understanding of the students I was serving. Well worth my time, I've always thought. It is also a chance for me to bring my own family!

By the end of the year, families know each other and have a sense of community. They look forward to coming to the end-of-year gathering. You experience the acknowledgment of your own continued efforts through the many hugs, handshakes, positive comments, and thank-yous these very grateful parents bestow upon you. They will have recognized the powerful program on which you worked so hard. They will see differences in their children. They will want to know, "Why couldn't school have been like this when I was a kid?"

The answer is simple. We are learning more and more about learning theory and the brain's capabilities. Good teachers have used many of these strategies for years. We now have the research to support, guide, and encourage us to orchestrate learner-centered classrooms with the brain in mind!

WHERE TO BEGIN

1. Begin to offer choices that address all eight intelligences in your teaching. Help your students become aware of their own strengths and areas that are developing.

2. Ask students to begin keeping daily journals in which they record the agenda and note their own goals for the day. Allow time at the end of the day or at the end of each lesson for self-reflection, processing, and assessment.

3. Select a few of the life skills for success on which to focus each month. Rich's (2008) book, *MegaSkills: Building Our Children's Character and Achievement for School and Life,* and the information online (http://wwwmegaskillshsi.org) will give you ideas for teaching some of the concepts. Create recognition certificates for students who exhibit the Life Skills you are working on.

4. Consider planning just one learning celebration during the year as a culminating event to a unit. Invite parents and the community. Experience your own success, as well.

Two Tools for the Learner-Centered Classroom

Life Skills for Success

Respect	To honor self, others, and the environment
Responsibility	To be accountable for one's own actions
Loyalty	To be devoted and faithful to family, friends, and country
Peace	To be calm and serene, not quarrelsome or violent
Cooperation	To work together toward a common goal or purpose
Integrity	To be honest, upright, and of sound moral principle and character
Kindness	To be gentle and thoughtful toward others
Initiative	To do something because it needs to be done
Flexibility	To have the ability to alter plans when necessary
Perseverance	To continue in spite of difficulties
Organization	To plan, arrange, and implement in an orderly way
Sense of humor	To laugh and be playful without hurting others
Effort	To try your hardest and work tirelessly
Reliability	To be trustworthy and dependable
Self-control	To have command over one's own actions and feelings
Common sense	To use good judgment
Problem solving	To create or seek solutions in difficult situations
Decision making	To have strategies for making up one's mind and forming opinions
Motivation	To want to do something and to be willing to move into action
Patience	To wait calmly for someone or something
Friendship	To make and keep a friend through mutual trust and caring
Curiosity	To desire to learn or know about a full range of things
Citizenship	To behave as a supportive, contributing member of a country or community

Eight Kinds of Smart

Student Checklist

Multiple intelligences include common skills that people have and that they use to process information and solve problems. Which are your strongest intelligences and your least developed? Check those statements that apply to you most often to find out.

Verbal-Linguistic: Word Smart

_____Books are important to me.

_____I have a pretty easy time memorizing poems, stories, facts, and so on.

_____I enjoy talking and telling stories.

_____I enjoy games such as Scrabble, Boggle, and hangman.

_____I like to write in a journal or to write stories.

_____I like to look things up in books and encyclopaedias.

_____I like to listen to people read aloud to me.

_____When I ride in a car, I like to read signs or play the ABC game.

_____I enjoy tongue twisters, rhymes, and puns.

_____I like to use big words when I write or speak.

Logical-Mathematical: Logic Smart

_____I enjoy counting things.

_____I like to make patterns, and I notice patterns in the world.

_____I often ask adults questions about the way things work.

_____I can add and subtract in my head.

_____I like to measure, sort, and organize things.

_____I like to play games or solve problems that require logical thinking.

_____I am interested in new inventions and theories in science.

_____I like to set up little experiments.

_____I enjoy doing math at school.

_____I like watching science shows on TV.

Visual-Spatial: Picture Smart

_____I enjoy drawing and painting pictures and designs.

_____I love colors, and I have some special favorites.

(Continued)

(Continued)

_____I enjoy putting together puzzles.

_____I like playing with blocks, Legos, Tinker Toys, and so on.

_____I have vivid and colorful dreams.

_____I can close my eyes and visualize things in my head.

_____I can usually find my way around my neighborhood or town.

_____I like to take pictures or videos.

_____I love to look at picture books or magazines that have a lot of photographs.

_____I can pick and match clothes to create great outfits.

Bodily-Kinesthetic: Body Smart

_____I play at least one sport on a regular basis.

_____I find it difficult to sit still for long periods of time.

_____I like working with my hands, doing activities such as building, weaving, carving, and so on.

_____I am well coordinated.

_____I need to touch things to learn more about them.

_____I love wild rides at the amusement park and other thrilling experiences.

_____I often spend my free time outside.

_____I like to ride a bike, skateboard, or skate.

_____I enjoy dancing.

_____I can act out things and imitate other people's movements.

Musical-Rhythmic: Music Smart

_____I have a pretty good singing voice.

_____I can tell when someone sings or plays a wrong or off-key note.

_____I like to play or would like to learn to play a musical instrument.

_____I like to listen to music on the radio, or on CDs or audiocassettes.

_____I sometimes catch myself humming a tune when I am working or learning.

_____I love to have music in my life.

_____I like to tap or bang on things to keep up a rhythm.

_____I've actually made up some of my own songs or music.

_____I notice nonverbal sounds (dogs barking, waves breaking, and so on) and hear things pretty well.

_____I sometimes get a melody or advertisement jingle stuck in my head.

Naturalist: Nature Smart

_____I love nature, animals, and the outdoors.

_____I can sense and notice patterns in nature; I enjoy pointing them out to others.

_____I am able to use patterns to navigate (get around); I am not afraid of getting lost in nature or a new environment.

_____I am sensitive to the changes in seasons, noon phases, tides, star patterns, and so on.

_____I am interested in learning the names and characteristics of various plants and animals.

_____I enjoy watching nature shows and shows about exploration and cultures different from my own.

_____I find it fascinating, not frightening, to be in environments different from my own.

_____I enjoy watching natural phenomena such as comets, sunsets, thunderstorms, and waves.

_____I blend in easily with nature or a new culture; sometimes I feel more comfortable in those environments than in my own.

_____I often want to be out in nature when I am thinking about something or solving a problem.

Interpersonal: People Smart

_____I usually have an easy time making friends.

_____I am a good at helping others solve problems.

_____I often want to help others.

_____I usually know what is going on with my friends and family.

_____I am often a leader in clubs or cooperative learning groups.

_____I am the kind of person who others seem to come to for advice.

_____I prefer group sports to individual ones.

_____I like playing games with others more than playing on my own.

_____I feel comfortable in crowds and at social gatherings.

_____I notice when people are upset or having a hard time.

Intrapersonal: Self Smart

_____I am pretty independent; I don't rely that much on others.

_____I have hobbies that I like to do on my own.

(Continued)

_____Sometimes I have opinions or ideas that set me apart from others.

_____I like to keep a diary or journal.

_____I prefer spending time alone in the woods to spending time at a busy, fancy resort.

_____I prefer playing games by myself (video games, solitaire) to playing with others.

_____I have some important ideas or goals that I like to think about.

_____I need time to work on things by myself rather than in a cooperative group.

_____I have a secret place or fort to which I retreat to get away from others.

_____I sometimes have a difficult time talking with others in a small group.

Epilogue

Develop Your "Teaching Compass"

The complex art of teaching is much more than content knowledge and instructional methodology. Each day in a classroom involves observation, conversation, reflection, improvisation, and innovation. There are always multiple "adjustment opportunities" within each lesson. The ability to anticipate what the next interaction should be for each student is a gift for some teachers, but it is an acquired skill that many of us must develop.

The National Board for Professional Teaching Standards lists five core principals that teachers should know and be able to do. The first standard is simply stated: "Teachers are committed to students and their learning." The standard states that teachers:

- Act on the belief that all students can learn;
- Treat students equitably, recognizing the individual differences that distinguish one student from another and taking account of these differences in their practice;
- Adjust their practice based on observation and knowledge of their students' interests, abilities, skills, knowledge, family circumstances, and peer relationships;
- Understand how students develop and learn;
- Incorporate the prevailing theories of cognition and intelligence in their practice;
- Are aware of the influence of context and culture on behavior;

- Develop students' cognitive capacity and their respect for learning; and
- Foster students' self-esteem, motivation, character, and civic responsibility.

Adapted from National Board for Professional Teaching Standards, 2002.

To manifest this standard in practice is a huge undertaking that requires teachers to have a guiding pedagogy. I call this your *teaching compass*. A compass is a consistent and true indicator of physical direction. It provides information so that you can calculate decisions about what direction you should take. Not only will a dynamic teacher have a tackle box of strategies to draw from, she will also have a belief system about children and learning that informs and guides her daily instructional decisions. As situations emerge in the classroom, your personal teaching compass can help you find your way through.

Begin with the brain. Understanding how brains learn, react under stress, and respond to experiences can help you develop your teaching compass. When each adjustment opportunity presents itself, I recommend that you turn to your growing knowledge about the brain and the field of cognitive neuroscience. By knowing about instructional practices designed to be most compatible with how children's brains learn naturally and most efficiently, you will be able to determine what strategy or process will be the best direction to take. As you design lessons, ask yourself the following questions:

- Will this strategy be too intimidating for this learner (i.e., be perceived as a threat)?
- Have I included clear procedures, so that the learner knows the expected behaviors?
- Does the classroom environment promote learning, exploration, and reflection?
- Does the classroom climate feel safe and secure?
- Have the students' basic needs been met?
- Would this learner benefit from some movement opportunities?
- Is the classroom a joyful place to be? Have we laughed recently?

- How might I modify, adapt, or extend this lesson to better suit this student's current capabilities?
- Are there opportunities for student choice?
- Will students be able to get immediate feedback as they learn?

What will your classroom be like a year from now? Where are you headed? What additional knowledge will you use as your teaching compass? As a life-long learner, examine your current practices and repertoire and seek to expand your knowledge and understanding about brain-compatible teaching and learning. I wish you well on your journey.

Bibliography

Amir, O. (2008, July 22). Tough choices: How making decisions tires your brain. *Scientific American: Mind Matters.* Retrieved July 18, 2009, from http://www.scientificamerican.com/article.cfm?id=tough-choices-how-making

Apple, M. W., & Beane, J. A. (Eds.). (1995). *Democratic schools.* Alexandria, VA: Association for Supervision and Curriculum Development.

Armstrong, T. (1999). *7 kinds of smart + 2.* New York: Penguin.

Armstrong, T. (2000). *In their own way: Discovering and encouraging your child's multiple intelligences* (Rev. ed.). New York: Tarcher/Putnam.

Armstrong, T. (2009). *Multiple intelligences in the classroom* (3rd ed.). Alexandria, VA: Association for Supervision and Curriculum Development.

Baratta-Lorton, M. (1976). *Mathematics their way.* Menlo Park, CA: Addison-Wesley.

Begley, S. (2007). *Train your mind, change your brain: How a new science reveals our extraordinary potential to transform ourselves.* New York: Ballantine Books.

Belvel, P. S., & Jordan, M. M. (2003). *Rethinking classroom management.* Thousand Oaks, CA: Corwin Press.

Bently, M. J. (n.d.). *Lighting the learning space* [Brochure]. Houston, TX: 3D/I. Retrieved July 18, 2009, from http://www.3di.com/toolbox/k12_pm/docstemplates/rd_lighting.pdf

Blakemore, S. J., & Frith, U. (2005). *The learning brain: Lessons for education.* Malden, MA: Blackwell.

Brookhart, S. M. (2008). *How to give effective feedback to your students.* Alexandria, VA: Association for Supervision and Curriculum Development.

Brooks, J. G., & Brooks, M. G. (1999). *The case for constructivist classrooms.* Alexandria, VA: Association for Supervision and Curriculum Development.

Caine, R. N., & Caine, G. (1994). *Making connections: Teaching and the human brain.* Menlo Park, CA: Addison-Wesley.

Caine, R. N., Caine, G., McClintic, C., & Klimek, K. (2005). *12 brain/mind learning principles in action.* Thousand Oaks, CA: Corwin Press.

Checkley, Kathy. 1998. No room for control. *Education Update* 40(6), 4–7.

Collaborative for the Advancement of Social and Emotional Learning (CASEL). (1997). *Promoting social and emotional learning: Guidelines for educators.* Alexandria, VA: Association for Supervision and Curriculum Development.

Committee on Developments in the Science of Learning, & Committee on Learning Research and Educational Practice. (2000). *How people learn: Brain, mind, experience and school.* Washington, DC: National Academy Press.

Csikszentmihalyi, M. (1990). *Flow: The psychology of optimal experience.* New York: HarperCollins.

Dewey, J. (1916). *Democracy and education.* New York: Macmillan.

Dickerson, V. (1997). *If problems talked.* Cupertino, CA: Guilford Press.

DiGiulio, R. (1995). *Positive classroom management.* Thousand Oaks, CA: Corwin Press.

Encyclopedia of childhood and adolescence. (2005–2006). *Learned helplessness.* Thomson Gale. Retrieved July 9, 2009, from http://www.bookrags.com/research/learned-helplessness-geca

Faber, A., & Mazlish, E. (1999). *How to talk so kids will listen and listen so kids will talk.* New York: HarperCollins.

Feinstein, S. (Ed.). (2007). *Learning and the brain: A comprehensive guide for educators, parents, and teachers.* Lanham, MD: Rowman & Littlefield.

Gardner, H. (1983). *Frames of mind.* New York: Harper and Row.

Gazzaniga, M. S. (2008). *HUMAN: The science behind what makes us unique.* New York: HarperCollins.

Gibbs, J. (1995). *Tribes: A new way of learning and being together.* Santa Rosa, CA: Center Source.

Gibbs, J. (2006). *Tribes learning communities.* Santa Rosa, CA: Center Source.

Glasser, W. (1986). *Control theory in the classroom.* New York: Harper and Row.

Glasser, W. (1998). *Choice theory: A new psychology of personal freedom.* New York: HarperCollins.

Goldberg, E. (2001). *The executive brain: Frontal lobes and the civilized mind.* New York: Oxford University Press.

Goleman, D. (2006). *Social intelligence: The new science of human relationships.* New York: Bantam.

Hannaford, C. (2005). *Smart moves* (Rev. ed.). New York: Midpoint Trade Books.

Hart, Leslie. 1998. *Human brain and human learning* (Rev. ed.). Kent, WA: Books for Educators.

HighScope Educational Research Foundation. (2009). *About us.* Retrieved July 23, 2009, from http://www.highscope.org/Content.asp?ContentId=6

Hopkin, K. (2007, November 19). Any choice is a good choice. *Scientific American.* Retrieved July 18, 2009, from http://www.scientificamerican.com/podcast/episode.cfm?id=4AC17780-E7F2-99DF-3C4AE9D48A9C13D3

Iacoboni, M. (2008). *Mirroring people: The new science of how we connect with others.* New York: Farrar, Straus and Giroux.

Institute of Education Sciences. (2008, September). *Reducing behavior problems in the elementary school classroom.* U.S. Department of Education. Retrieved July 18, 2009, from http://ies.ed.gov/ncee/wwc/pdf/practiceguides/behavior_pg_092308.pdf

Jensen, E. (2000). *Brain-based learning* (Rev. ed.). Thousand Oaks, CA: Corwin Press.

Jensen, E. (2003). *Tools for engagement.* Thousand Oaks, CA: Corwin Press.

Jensen, E. (2005). *Teaching with the brain in mind* (2nd ed.). Alexandria, VA: Association for Supervision and Curriculum Development.

Jensen, E. (2006). *Enriching the brain.* San Francisco: Jossey-Bass.

Jensen, E., & Dabney, M. (2000). *Learning smarter: The new science of teaching.* Thousand Oaks, CA: Corwin Press.

Johnson, S., & Johnson, C. (1988). *The one-minute teacher.* New York: William and Morrow.

Kagan, M., Kagan, L., & Kagan, S. (1999). *Classbuilding.* San Clemente, CA: Kagan.

Kagan, S., & Kagan, M. (1998). *Multiple intelligences: The complete MI book.* San Clemente, CA: Kagan Cooperative Learning.

Kandel, E. R. (2006). *In search of memory: The emergence of a new science of mind.* New York: W.W. Norton & Co.

Kohn, A. (1999). *Punished by rewards.* Boston: Houghton Mifflin.

Kohn, A. (2006). *Beyond discipline: From compliance to community.* Alexandria, VA: Association for Supervision and Curriculum Development.

Lazear, D. (1999). *Eight ways of knowing: Teaching for multiple intelligences.* Arlington Heights, IL: Skylight.

Ledoux, J. (1996). *The emotional brain: The mysterious underpinnings of emotional life.* New York: Touchstone.

Ledoux, J. (2002). *Synaptic self.* New York: Penguin Group.

Lewis, B. (2000). *The kid's guide to social action* (Rev. ed.). Minneapolis, MN: Free Spirit.

Lickona, T. (1992). *Educating for character.* New York: Bantam.

Lowery, L. (1989). *Thinking and learning: Matching developmental stages with curriculum and instruction.* Pacific Grove, CA: Midwest.

MacDonald, M. (2008). *Your brain: The missing manual.* Sebastapol, CA: Pogue Press.

Margulies, N., & Sylwester, R. (1998). *Emotion and attention.* Tucson, AZ: Zephyr Press.

Marzano, R. J. (2007). *The art and science of teaching.* Alexandria, VA: Association for Supervision and Curriculum Development.

McCombs, B. L., & Miller, L. (2007). *Learner-centered classroom practices and assessments.* Thousand Oaks, CA: Corwin Press.

McKhann, G., & Albert, M. (2002). *Keep your brain young.* Hoboken, NJ: DANA Press, John Wiley & Sons.

Medina, J. (2008). *Brain rules: 12 principles for surviving and thriving at work, home, and school.* Seattle, WA: Pear Press.

Miller, N. (Ed.). (1995). *The healthy school handbook: Conquering the sick building syndrome and other environmental hazards in and around your school.* Washington, DC: National Education Association.

Monarch opens clean-up exhibit. (2008, September 28). *Santa Cruz Sentinel.* Retrieved July 13, 2009, from http://www.scsextra.com/story.php?sid=79824

National Board for Professional Teaching Standards. (2002). *What teachers should know and be able to do* [Brochure]. Arlington, VA: Author.

Nelsen, J., Lott, L., & Glenn, H. S. (2000). *Positive discipline in the classroom* (3rd ed.). New York: Three Rivers Press.

Nelsen, J., & Lott, L. (1994). *Positive discipline for teenagers* (2nd ed.). New York: Three Rivers Press.

Ornstein, R. (1991). *The evolution of consciousness.* New York: Simon & Schuster.

Parsons Corporation. (2008). *Educational facilities.* Retrieved July 9, 2009, from http://www.parsons.com/infra/education/default.asp

PBIS. (2009). What is school-wide positive behavioral interventions & supports? *OSEP technical assistance center on positive behavioral interventions & supports.* Retrieved July 18, 2009, from http://www.pbis.org/school/what_is_swpbs.aspx

Pearson, H. (2003, December 4). Jokes activate brain reward region. *BioEd Online.* Retrieved July 18, 2009, from http://www.bioedonline.org/news/news.cfm?art=624

Pert, C. (1999). *Molecules of emotion: Why you feel the way you feel.* New York: Touchstone.

Posner, M. I., & Rothbart, M. (2007). *Educating the human brain.* Washington, DC: American Psychological Association.

Ratey, J. J. (2002). *A user's guide to the brain.* New York: Vintage Books.

Ratey, J. (2008). *SPARK: The revolutionary new science of exercise and the brain.* New York: Little, Brown, and Company.

Rich, D. (1988). *MegaSkills: How families can help children succeed in school and beyond.* Boston: Houghton Mifflin.

Rich, D. (2008). *MegaSkills: Building our children's character and achievement for school and life.* Boston: Houghton Mifflin.

Slavin, R. (1994). *A practical guide to cooperative learning.* Boston: Allyn and Bacon.

Smith, F. (1986). *Insult to intelligence.* New York: Arbor House.

Sousa, D. A. (2005). *How the brain learns* (3rd ed.). Thousand Oaks, CA: Corwin Press.

Sousa, D. A. (2009). *How the brain influences behavior.* Thousand Oaks, CA: Corwin Press.

Striker, S. (1983a). *The anti-coloring book.* New York: Henry Holt.

Striker, S. (1983b). *The anti-coloring book of masterpieces.* New York: Henry Holt.

Striker, S. (1983c). *The mystery anti-coloring book.* New York: Henry Holt.

Sylwester, R. (1998). The downshifting dilemma. Unpublished paper.

Tate, M. (2003). *Worksheets don't grow dendrites: 20 instructional strategies that engage the brain.* Thousand Oaks, CA: Corwin Press.

U.S. Environmental Protection Agency. (2007, October). *Healthy school environmental assessment tool.* Retrieved July 9, 2009, from http://www.epa.gov/schools/healthyseat

Venolia, C. (1988). *Healing environments.* Berkeley, CA: Celestial Arts.

Willis, J. (2007). *Brain-friendly strategies for the inclusion classroom.* Alexandria, VA: Association for Supervision and Curriculum Development.

Wolfe, P. (2001). *Brain matters: Translating research into classroom practice.* Alexandria, VA: Association for Supervision and Curriculum Development.

Wong, H., & Wong, R. T. (2009). *The First Days of School* (4th ed.). Mountain View, CA: Wong.

Zull, J. E. (2002). *The art of changing the brain.* Sterling, VA: Stylus.

Recommended Reading

Aamodt, S., & Wang, S. (2008). *Welcome to your brain.* New York: Bloomsbury USA.

Allen, R. (2008). *Green light classrooms: Teaching techniques that accelerate learning.* Thousand Oaks, CA: Corwin Press.

Belvel, P. S., & Jordan, M. M. (2003). *Rethinking classroom management.* Thousand Oaks, CA: Corwin Press.

Blakemore, S. J., & Frith, U. (2005). *The learning brain: Lessons for education.* Malden, MA: Blackwell.

Brown, S. (2009). *Play: How it shapes the brain, opens the imagination, and invigorates the soul.* New York: Avery/Penguin.

Caine, G., Caine, R. N., & Crowell, S. (1999). *MindShifts: A brain-based process for restructuring schools and renewing education* (Rev. ed.). Tucson, AZ: Zephyr Press.

Caine, R. N., Caine, G., McClintic, C., & Klimek, K. (2005). *12 brain/mind learning principles in action.* Thousand Oaks, CA: Corwin Press.

Csikszentmihalyi, M. (1990). *Flow: The psychology of optimal experience.* New York: HarperCollins.

D'Arcangelo, M. (Producer/Writer), & Nieboer, L. (Director). (1998). New knowledge and understanding [Video series, tape 1]. *The brain & learning.* Alexandria, VA: Association for Supervision and Curriculum Development.

Denton, P. (2005). *Learning through academic choice.* Turners Falls, MA: Northeast Foundation for Children.

DiGiulio, R. (1995). *Positive classroom management.* Thousand Oaks, CA: Corwin Press.

Elias, M. J., Zins, J. E., Weissberg, R. P., Frey, K. S., Greenberg, M. T., Haynes, M. M., et al. (1997). *Promoting social and emotional learning: Guidelines for educators.* Alexandria, VA: Association for Supervision and Curriculum Development.

Erlauer, L. (2003). *The brain-compatible classroom.* Alexandria, VA: Association for Supervision and Curriculum Development.

Faber, A., & Mazlish, E. (1999). *How to talk so kids can learn.* New York: Simon & Schuster.

Glasser, W. (1986). *Control theory in the classroom.* New York: Harper and Row.

Glenn, H. S., & Nelson, J. (2000). *Raising self-reliant children in a self-indulgent world* (2nd ed.). New York: Random House.

Goleman, D. (2005). *Emotional intelligence: Why it can matter more than IQ.* New York: Bantam.

Grant, J., Johnson, B., & Richardson, I. (1996). *Our best advice: The multiage problem solving handbook.* Peterborough, NH: Crystal Springs.

Greenfield, S. A. (1997). *The human brain: A guided tour.* New York: Basic Books.

Gregory, G., & Chapman, C. (2002). *Differentiated instructional strategies: One size doesn't fit all.* Thousand Oaks, CA: Corwin Press.

Gregory, G. & Parry, T. (2006). *Designing brain-compatible learning* (3rd ed.). Thousand Oaks, CA: Corwin Press.

Harris, J. M. (1989). *You and your child's self-esteem.* New York: Warner.

Healy, J. (1999). *Endangered minds.* New York: Simon & Schuster.

Healy, J. (2004). *Your child's growing mind.* New York: Broadway Books.

Jensen, E. (1997). *Completing the brain-compatible puzzle* (2nd ed.). Del Mar, CA: The Brain Store.

Jensen, E. (2005). *Teaching with the brain in mind* (2nd ed.). Alexandria, VA: Association for Supervision and Curriculum Development.

Jensen, E. (2008). *Brain-based learning* (2nd ed.). Thousand Oaks, CA: Corwin Press.

Kaufeldt, M. (2005). *Teachers, change your bait! Brain-compatible differentiated instruction.* Williston, VT: Crown House.

Kohn, A. (2006). *Beyond discipline: From compliance to community.* Alexandria, VA: Association for Supervision and Curriculum Development.

Kovalik, S., & Olsen, K. (2001). *Exceeding expectations: A users guide to implementing brain research in the classroom.* Black Diamond, WA: Books for Educators.

Lazear, D. (2003). *Eight ways of teaching: The artistry of teaching with multiple intelligences.* Thousand Oaks, CA: Corwin Press.

Ledoux, J. (1996). *The emotional brain: The mysterious underpinnings of emotional life.* New York: Touchstone.

Levine, M. (2002). *A mind at a time.* New York: Simon & Schuster.

Louv, R. (2008). *Last child in the woods: Saving our children from nature-deficit disorder.* Chapel Hill, NC: Algonquin Books.

Margulies, N. (2001). *Mapping inner space: Learning and teaching mind mapping* (2nd ed.). Thousand Oaks, CA: Corwin Press.

Marzano, R. J. (2007). *The art and science of teaching.* Alexandria, VA: Association for Supervision and Curriculum Development.

McCombs, B. L., & Miller, L. (2007). *Learner-centered classroom practices and assessments.* Thousand Oaks, CA: Corwin Press.

Nelson, C., de Haan, M., & Thomas, K. M. (2006). *Neuroscience of cognitive development.* Hoboken, NJ: John Wiley & Sons.

Politano, C., & Paquin, J. (2000). *Brain-based learning with class.* Winnipeg, Manitoba, Canada: Portage & Main.

Porro, B. (1996). *Talk it out: Conflict resolution in the elementary classroom.* Alexandria, VA: Association for Supervision and Curriculum Development.

Posner, M. I., & Rothbart, M. (2007). *Educating the human brain.* Washington, DC: American Psychological Association.

Ratey, J. J. (2002). *A user's guide to the brain.* New York: Vintage Books.

Ratey, J. (2008). *SPARK: The revolutionary new science of exercise and the brain.* New York: Little, Brown, and Company.

Schwartz, B. (2004, March). The tyranny of choice. *Scientific American.* Retrieved July 18, 2009, from http://www.scientificamerican.com/article.cfm?id=the-tyranny-of-choice-2004-04

Sprenger, M. (2008). *The developing brain: Birth to age eight.* Thousand Oaks, CA: Corwin Press.

Sylwester, R. (1995). *A celebration of neurons.* Alexandria, VA: Association for Supervision and Curriculum Development.

Sylwester, R. (2004). *How to explain a brain.* Thousand Oaks, CA: Corwin Press.

Sylwester, R. (2007). *The adolescent brain.* Thousand Oaks, CA: Corwin Press.

Venolia, C. (1988). *Healing environments.* Berkeley, CA: Celestial Arts.

Willis, J. (2008). *How your child learns best: Brain-friendly strategies you can use to ignite your child's learning and increase school success.* Napierville, IL: Sourcebooks.

Wolfe, P. (2001). *Brain matters: Translating research into classroom practice.* Alexandria, VA: Association for Supervision and Curriculum Development.

Wong, H., & Wong, R. T. (2005). *The first days of school.* Mountain View, CA: Wong.

Zapolsky, R. M. (1999). *Why zebras don't get ulcers.* New York: Freeman & Co.

Index

CORWIN

A SAGE Company

The Corwin logo—a raven striding across an open book—represents the union of courage and learning. Corwin is committed to improving education for all learners by publishing books and other professional development resources for those serving the field of PreK–12 education. By providing practical, hands-on materials, Corwin continues to carry out the promise of its motto: **"Helping Educators Do Their Work Better."**